FOREWORD

Praise and Worship Songbook Sixteen includes all of the songs from the f

I Will Sing
Never Gonna Stop
Lion Of Judah
Dwell In The House
Come Heal This Land
Open Up The Sky

Every song is arranged with vocal parts corresponding to the recording, which can easily be performed by your choir or worship team. The piano parts have been simplified from the recording, but follow the basic arrangement.

Musicians should be encouraged to embellish these arrangements by improvising with the chord symbols. When there is a note under a slash (e.g., F/G), the note above the slash is the chord to be played by the upper register instruments (guitar, right hand of the piano, etc.). The note below the slash is to be played by the lower register instruments (bass guitar, organ pedals, left hand of the piano, etc.). For songs that flow smoothly with each other, a medley reference is listed on each appropriate page.

This songbook has many features to help you plan your worship services.

Index "A" lists all songs by key and tempo. Praise and worship times will flow more smoothly if you select songs that are closely related in key and tempo. Create medleys of songs rather than stopping after each song. Choose songs that are related thematically, such as:

Here We Are	F Major, G Major
Have Your Way	G Major
We Wait	D Major

Index "B" lists the songs by topic, such as joy, thanksgiving, victory, etc. If you know the theme of your pastor's message, you can prepare the hearts of the people by focusing your worship on the same topic.

Index "C" lists songs by the first line of lyrics in case you are unsure of the title.

Index "D" lists the songs according to their Scriptural references. If you are searching for a song featuring a specific Scripture, you will find it listed in Biblical order.

Index "E" lists copyright owners of the songs presented in this publication.

We wish to thank all those who have given their permission to print the songs in this book. Every effort has been made to locate the copyright owners. If any omissions have occurred, we will make proper corrections in future printings. The words of the songs in this book may only be reproduced by obtaining permission from the copyright owner of the individual song. For information concerning or obtaining a CCLI License (Christian Copyright License International), please call them at (800) 234-2446 or logging on to www.ccli.com.

Transcribed by Ed Kerr. Compiled by Luke Gambill and Rhonda Scelsi.

www.integritymusic.com

TABLE OF CONTENTS

...The anointing you received from him remains in you... 1 John 2:27 (NIV)

A New Anointing

Words and Music by
DAVID BARONI

12
O Lord, let it pour;
A
E/G♯
B
C♯m/B
A/B
16
A new a - noint -
E
E/G♯
ing for a new day,
A
B
C♯m
20
to car - ry the glo - ry of the Lord,
F♯m7
B 7sus
C♯m

24
to car - ry the glo - ry of the Lord.
C♯m/B
F♯m7
B 7sus
1, 2.
Worship Leader
28
VERSE
The oil from yes - ter - day
Esus
E
B/D♯
has grown stale, and the
A/C♯
E
32
strength that I once trust - ed in has failed;
B/D♯
A/C♯
Bsus

36
But Your fresh Word has been spo - ken, and my proud
B
E/G♯
A
D
heart has been bro - ken, Lord; So, once a-gain I
40
A
Esus
E
F♯m7
come be-hind the veil ask - ing for a
E/G♯
Bsus
B
3.
45
BRIDGE
W.L.
Ho - ly fra - grance,
E
E/G♯
E/A

49
sweet per-fume, all con-sum - ing fire
B 7sus
E
D2
(re) fill this room;
A/C♯
E
Esus
E
E2
E
53
No more liv - ing in yes - ter - day's grace;
F♯m7
E/G♯
D2
57
O Lord, pour out Your pow - er and Your pas -
E
F♯m7
E/G♯
A

sion for Your pur - pos - es to-day.
E/B
C♯m7
Bsus
63
CHORUS
P.T.
W.L. ad libs
New a-noint - ing for a new day,
F
F/A
B♭
B♭/C
F
67
O Lord, let it pour;
B♭
F/A
71
A new a-noint -
C
Dm/C
C
B♭/C
F
F/A

ing for a new day,
B♭
C
Dm
75
to car - ry the glo - ry of the Lord,
Gm7
C 7sus
Dm
79
to car - ry the glo - ry of
Dm/C
Gm7
C 7sus
1.
2.
the Lord,
C 7sus

Medley options: Thine is The Kingdom; Surely Goodness And Mercy

I press on toward the goal to win the prize for which God has called me heavenward in Christ Jesus. Philippians 3:14 (NIV)

All The Way

Words and Music by
RONALD JOSHUA KENOLY

13
is the day that ev - 'ry - thing be - gan to change;
be - cause my faith in You is get - ting so
Dm
strong;
C2
Am7
17
The prob - lems that I faced
The peace and love from You,
Dm
were get - ting strong - er,
it keeps me stand - ing
Gm/D
I thought when I
through an - y - thing I
21
got saved
go through;
F/B♭
my prob - lems would go a - way;
I know that I can't lose
Dm7
Csus

25
But the change I made be - gan to real - ly
'cause the more I pray, the more I feel Your
Am7
29
take a toll on me, and when I told my friends a - bout
strength in - side of me, and the more I seek Your face,
Dm
Dm7
Am7(add4)
You, Lord, they laughed hy - ster - i - c'lly;
I find You're all I real - ly need;
But no
And this
Dm
33
mat - ter what they say or what they choose to think of me;
feel - ing that I feel I've nev - er felt since I've been free;
3
Am7
A♭dim7
Gm
3
3

37
I'm gon - na stay here strong for You, my Lord, no mat - ter
I'm gon - na stand here strong for You, my Lord, no mat - ter
B♭2
what the cost might be.
what the cost might be.
All
41
CHORUS
I'm gon - na serve You,
B♭2/C
F
W.L. ad libs
Praise Team
be - cause I love You;
I'm go - ing with
F2
Dm7
F2/D
45
You
all the way;
Gm7
C7sus

49
When friends for - sake me,
I won't let it break
C
Am7
53
me;
I'm go - ing with You
Dm7
D7
Gm7
1.
all the way,
all the way.
C 7sus
C
57
B♭m
F

Bbm
Bbm/Ab
F
W.L.
2.
P.T.
2. Now the
All the way,
C 7sus
66
CHORUS
W.L. ad libs
all the way;
F
F2
Dm7
70
all the way,
all the way;
F2/D
Gm7

Medley options: Use Me; You Are My All In All.

.... "Stand at the crossroads and look; ask for the ancient paths, ask where the good way is, and walk in it.... Jeremiah 6:16 (NIV)

Ancient Words

♩= 63

Words and Music by
LYNN DESHAZO

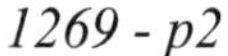

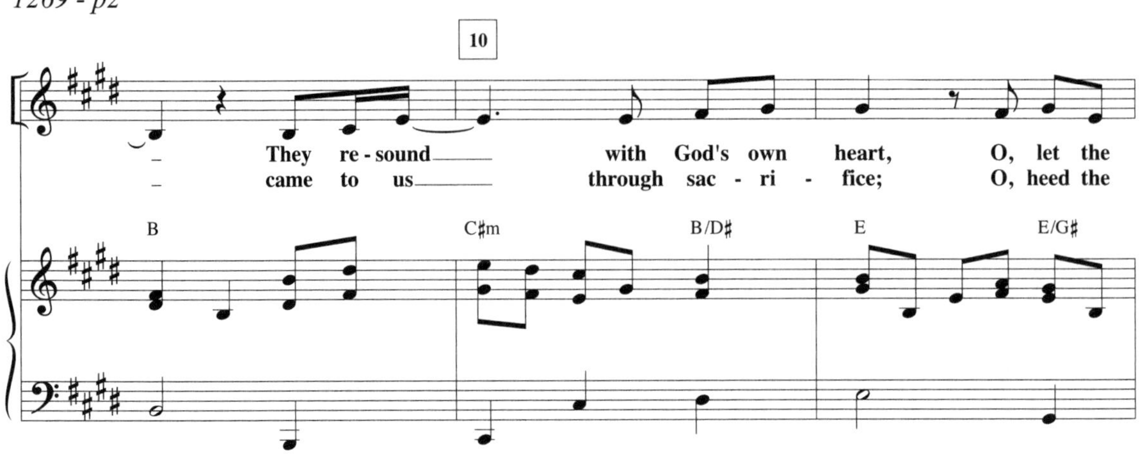
10
They re - sound with God's own heart, O, let the
came to us through sac - ri - fice; O, heed the
B
C♯m
B/D♯
E
E/G♯

an - cient words im - part; Words of
faith - ful words of Christ; Ho - ly
F♯m/A
E/B
B
E
Esus

15
life, words of hope, give us strength, help us cope;
words long pre - served for our walk in this world;
Praise Team
Oo,
Oo;
E
B
E
A

19
In this world where - 'er we roam, an-cient
They re - sound with God's own heart; O, let the
Oo,
B
C♯m
B/D♯
E
E/G♯
words will guide us home.
an - cient words im - part.
An - cient
Oo.
An - cient
F♯m/A
E/B
B
E
25
CHORUS
words, ev - er true, chang - ing me, chang - ing
words, ev - er true, chang - ing me, chang - ing
E
E/G♯
B
F♯m/A
E/G♯

29
you;
We have
come
with o - pen
hearts,
O let the
you;
Oo,
A
B
C♯m
B/D♯
E
1.
32
an - cient words
im
-
part.
An - cient words
im
-
part.
F♯m/A
E/B
B
E
B/D♯
E
E/G♯
36
W.L.
2. Ho - ly
A
E/B
B
E
A/E
E

2.
D.S.
an - cient words im - part. An - cient
An - cient words im - part. An - cient
F♯m/A
E/B
B
E
A/E
3.
an - cient words im - part. We have
An - cient words im - part.
F♯m/A
E/B
B
E
42
come with o - pen hearts, O let the an - cient words im -
Oo,
An - cient words im -
C♯m
B/D♯
E
E/G♯
F♯m/A
E/B
B

Medley options: Here Is Love; The Lord Is My Strength And My Song.

Now arise, O LORD God, and come to your resting place... 2 Chronicles 6:41 (NIV)

Arise, O Lord

Words and Music by
CRAIG SMITH

place of our Lord; Come and bow be-fore the Lord our God, Je-ho-vah;
pres-ence of the Lord, en-ter in and wor-ship the Lord, our God Je-ho-vah;
Cm Eb/Bb F Cm Eb/Bb F Ab Bb Cm
14 W.L. & Praise Team Men
Ev-'ry heart that yearns for the cham-bers of our King,
All, P.T. Men top note
Lift your hands in the sanc-tu-a-ry of our God;
Ab Bb Cm Cm Eb/Bb F Cm Eb/Bb F
en-ter in and hon-or our Lord, our God, Je-ho-vah.
All
A-
Lift your voice, ex-tol the Lord of Ma-jes-ty.
All
A-
Cm Eb/Bb F Ab Bb Cm Ab Bb Cm

19
CHORUS
rise, O Lord, come in-to Your rest-ing place; Your child-ren sing and wor-ship
Ab Bb Cm
23
God, our King; A-rise, O Lord, come in-to Your rest-ing place; With
27
joy we sing, we wor-ship God, our King, we wor-ship
F
1.
God, our King.
2.
God, our King; A-
D.S.
Cm Eb/Bb F F/A

Medley options: Let The Weight Of Your Glory Fall; All Consuming Fire.

Oh, worship the LORD in the beauty of holiness... Psalm 96:9 (NKJ)

As We Worship You

Words and Music by
TOMMY WALKER

hun - ger and a hope to those who've strayed so far. As we
Bm
G
D/F♯
10
CHORUS
bow in ad - o - ra - tion and stand in rev - 'rent awe, show Your
Em7
D/F♯
maj - es - ty and glo - ry, let Your a - noint - ing fall; As we de -
G
Asus
A
Bm
14
clare Your name, Lord Je - sus, as the on - ly name Who saves, may the
Em7
D/F♯

1.
pow'r of Your sal - va - tion fill each heart, we pray. As we
G
Asus
A
Bm
A/C♯
19
VERSE
W.L.
wor - ship You, let all the na - tions hear our song, the song of
P.T.
Oo;
D
A/C♯
Je - sus and His blood that proved His love for all; As we
As we
Bm
G

23
worship You, may all the lost and broken come; May they
worship You, Oo;
D
A/C♯
hear Your still small voice call out their names, each one.
All
As we
Bm
G
D/F♯
2. All
W.L.
29
VERSE
W.L.
As we worship You, let all the world
P.T.
As we worship You, Oo;
Bm
A/C♯
B♭/D
C/E
F

come and see how the mer - cy we've re - ceived from You can
C/E
Dm
33
3
set them free; As we wor - ship You, let all this joy that fills our hearts bring a
As we wor - ship You, Oo;
B♭
F
C/E
All
hun - ger and a hope to those who've strayed so far. As we
Dm
B♭
F/A

37 CHORUS

bow in ad-o-ra-tion and stand in rev-'rent awe, show Your

Gm7 F/A

maj-es-ty and glo-ry, let Your a-noint-ing fall; As we de-

B♭ Csus C Dm

41

clare Your name, Lord Je-sus, as the on-ly name Who saves, may the

Gm7 F/A

last time to Coda

pow'r of Your sal-va-tion fill each heart, we pray, as we

B♭ Csus C Dm C/E

Medley options: We Give You Glory; You Are Good

1272

...."I believe that Jesus Christ is the Son of God." Acts 8:37 (NKJ)

Behold The Son Of God

Words and Music by
ROBIN MARK

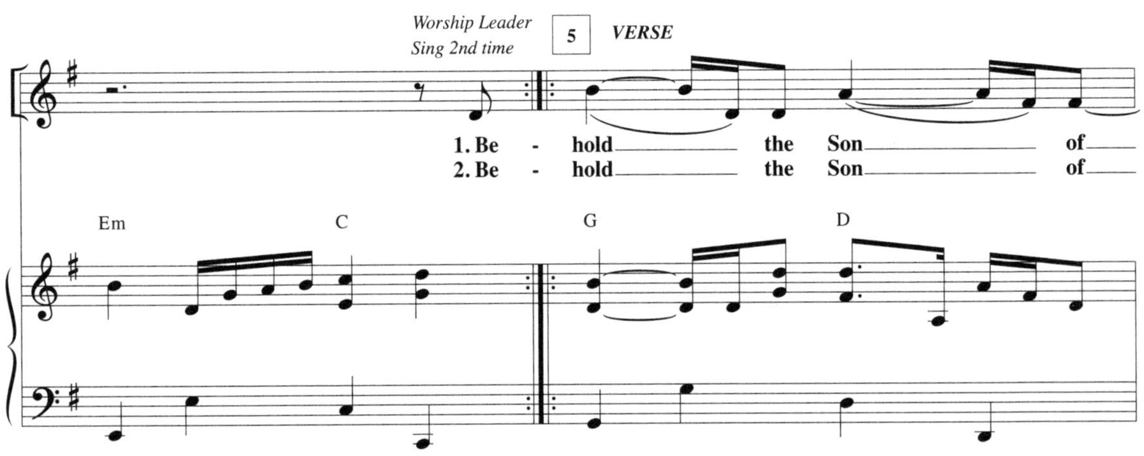

9
suf - fer - ing my pun - ish - ment; Sac - ri - fice of grace,
o - ver death vic - tor - i - ous, Heav - en's Prince of Peace,
Praise Team, 2nd time only
Oo, Oo,
Am G C G
though He dies yet shall He live for - ev -
though He died yet shall He live for - ev -
Oo, for - ev -
C G G/F
1st time All
2nd time W.L.
15
er; And here we stand, O
er; And we shall stand, O
Praise Team, 2nd time only
er. We shall stand, O
D Dsus D Dsus D G D

God, as tro - phies of Your
Lord, be - fore that throne of
Lord, be - fore that throne of
Em C G D
19
grace, drawn from dark - ness in - to light
grace, bought by Your re - deem - ing love,
Both times, Praise Team
grace; Oo,
Em C Am G
of Your Spir - it poured; Though we die yet shall we live for -
pur - chased by the blood; Though we die yet shall we live for -
Oo, Oo, for -
C G C G

22
All
ev - er.
ev - er.
There is
ev - er.
G/F
D Dsus D
Dsus D

25
CHORUS
no con-dem-na - tion now for those who put their trust in You a-lone; We wor -
C G D
Em C

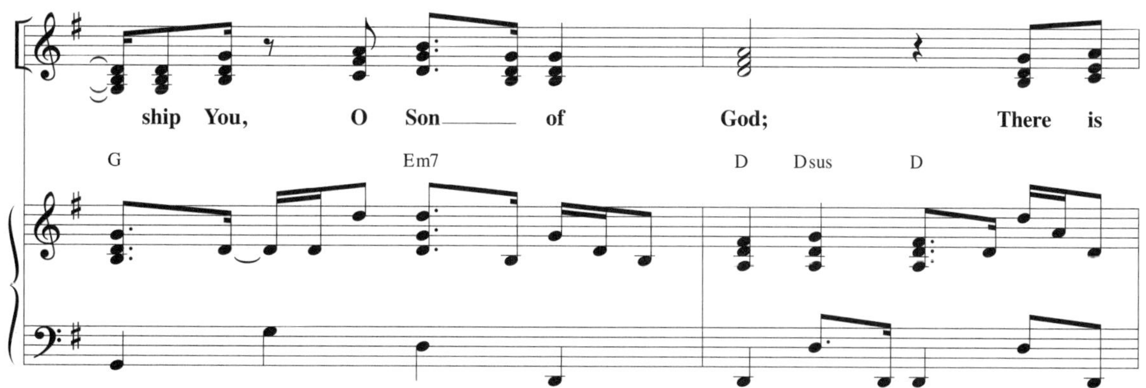
ship You, O Son of God; There is
G Em7
D Dsus D

Medley options: I Look To You; Unto You.

If my people, who are called by my name, will humble themselves and pray...then will I hear from heaven and will forgive their sin and will heal their land. 2 Chronicles 7:14 (NIV)

Come Heal This Land

Words and Music by
ROBIN MARK

11
1.
wid - ow'd ones, all you poor and dis - pos - sess'd;
Fa - ther's breast, where His mer - cy
F Am F G C
2.
rit.
2. For a is com - plete.
G C
16
A tempo
C G Am F
20
VERSE
W.L.
1. Does a cry ring out
2. Do the tears of One
3. So may this land we love
C G Am F C G

from a bro - ken na - tion, from a peo - ple who have been
Who gave all things for us, do they flow from Heav - en still
be a place of safe - ty, be a light for all the na -
Am
F
C
G
24
brought low;
be - cause of us;
tions of this earth;
Was pride in our hearts,
For we have tast - ed grace
May Your streams of love,
and did we grieve Your Spir - it, have we blocked the an - cient
and we have known Your mer - cy, but we have not shown this
may they flow here free - ly, here where ev - 'ry strang - er

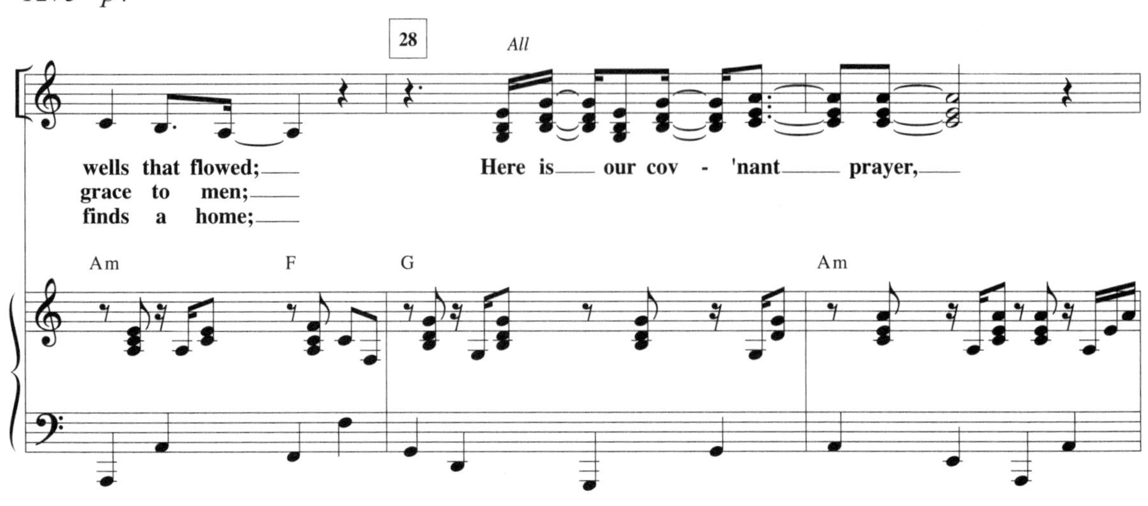
28
All
wells that flowed;
grace to men;
finds a home;
Here is our cov - 'nant prayer,
Am
F
G
Am

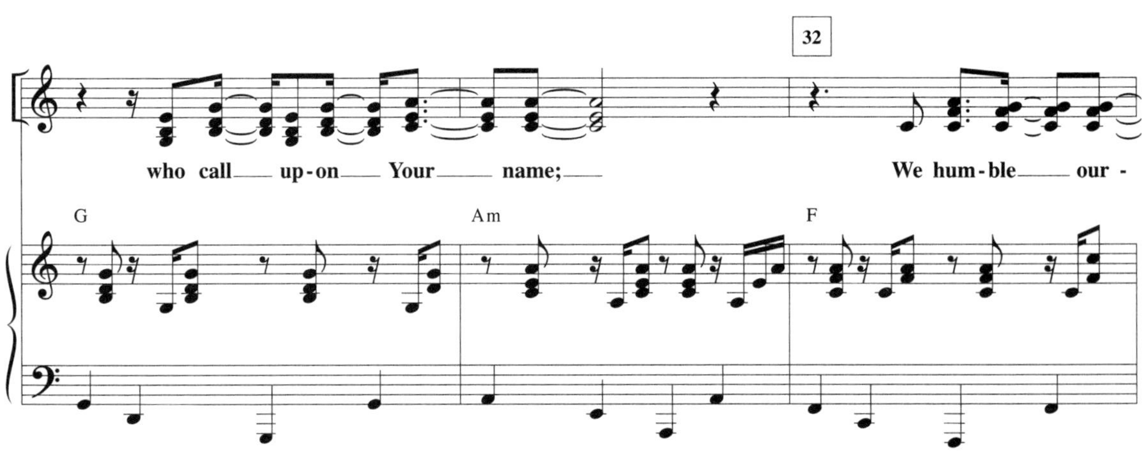
32
who call up-on Your name;
We hum-ble our -
G
Am
F

W.L.
All
selves be-fore You,
we hum-ble our - selves.
C
F
G

36
CHORUS
W.L.
Come heal this land; come heal this
Praise Team
Come heal this land; come heal this
Am G F Am G
40
land; come heal this land,
land; come heal this land,
F Am G F
1.
come heal this land.
come heal this land.
Am G F

2.
46
INSTRUMENTAL
land.
land.
F
C
G
Am
F
C
G
Am
F
50
Dm7
Am
F
C
Gsus
G
3.
55
CHORUS
land,
Come heal this land;
land,
Come heal this land;
F
Am
G
F

Medley options: Who Can Satisfy; When It's All Been Said And Done.

...Come, let us go up to the mountain of the LORD, to the house of the God of Jacob... Isaiah 2:3 (NIV)

Come Let's Go Up To The Mountain

Words and Music by
SUZY WILLIS and MATTHEW DONOVAN

king - dom,
shout - ing, they lay down their swords.
Zi - on will be called ho - ly for - ev - er - more.
D5
A
D5
13
CHORUS
All
Come, let's go up to the moun - tain,
come, let's go up to the Lord;
D5
C
Come, let's go up to the moun - tain, He will teach us His ways;
D5
C
G

17
Come, let's go up to the moun - tain,
come, let's go up to the Lord;
D5
C
Come, let's go up to the moun-tain, He will
teach us His ways.
2.
D.S.
teach us His ways.
D5
C
G
C
G
3.
teach us his ways.
C
G
D5
25
W.L.
A -
E5

27
VERSE
rise and shake the earth so might - i - ly, send Your glo - ry all a - cross the land;
E5
E5
31
Then ev - 'ry - thing that's proud and loft - y will bow
D2
A
E5
E5
down be - fore the Son of Man.
B
E5
35
CHORUS
All
Come, let's go up to the moun - tain, come, let's go up to the Lord;
E5
D

Come, let's go up to the moun - tain, He will teach us His ways;
E5
D
A
39
Come, let's go up to the moun - tain, come, let's go up to the Lord;
E5
D
last time to Coda
1.
Come, let's go up to the moun - tain, He will teach us His ways.
E5
D
A
2.
44
teach us His ways.
D
A
E5

46
BRIDGE
All
O - ver all the glo - ry there will be a co - ver - ing, a
E/B
C♯m
48
cloud of smoke all through the day, a flam - ing fire (re) all through the night, a
E5
ta - ber - na - cle for the shade, a shel - ter from the pour - ing rain,
E/B
C♯m
52
when the Lord has washed a - way the guilt from the daugh - ters of Zi - on.
E5

54
E5
D/F♯
E5
Dmaj7/F♯
E5
D/F♯
1, 2, 3.
4.
59
Come, come, come.
D5
D5
E5
D/F♯
D.S.S. al Coda
W.L.
A–
E5
Dmaj7/F♯
E5
Coda
64 CHORUS
teach us His ways.
Come, let's go up to the moun - tain,
D
A
E5

65
come, let's go up to the Lord;
Come, let's go up to the moun - tain, He will
D
E5
teach us His ways;
Come, let's go up to the moun - tain,
D
A
E5
69
come, let's go up to the Lord;
Come, let's go up to the moun - tain, He will
D
E5
72
teach us His ways.
D
A
E5
D2/E

Medley options: Crown Him With Many Crowns.

My beloved *is* mine, and I *am* his... Song of Solomon 2:16 (NKJ)

Dance With Me

Words and Music by
CHRIS DUPRÉ

14
W.L.
of my soul, to the song of all
G D/G A G
18
1st time W.L.
2nd time, W.L. and P.T. men
songs; Ro - mance
D Asus D Dsus2,4
me, O Lov - er of my
G/D D D/G G6(no3) G D/G
22
W.L.
soul, to the song of all songs.
A G D G/D

26
VERSE
W.L.
1. Be - hold You have come o - ver the hills,
2. With You I will go, You are my
Praise Team
Oo,
D
Bm
G
up - on the moun - tains;
love, You are my fair one;
30
To me You have
Win - ter is
Oo,
Oo,
D
Asus
A
Bm
1.
run, my be - loved;
You've cap - tur'd my
oo.
G
D

2.
heart.
past, and the
Asus
G
36
spring - time has come.
Oo. come.
D
Asus
A
39
CHORUS
All
Dance with me, O Lov - er
D
Dsus2,4
G/D
D
D/G
G6(no3)

43
of my soul, to the song of all
G D/G A G
songs;
47
Ro - mance
D Asus D Dsus2,4
me, O Lov - er of my
G/D D D/G G6(no3) G D/G
51
soul, to the song of all songs.
A G D

Medley options: Yahweh Is Holy.

Your love, O LORD, reaches to the heavens, your faithfulness to the skies. Psalm 36:5 (NIV)

Day After Day

Words and Music by
MIKE MOTLEY

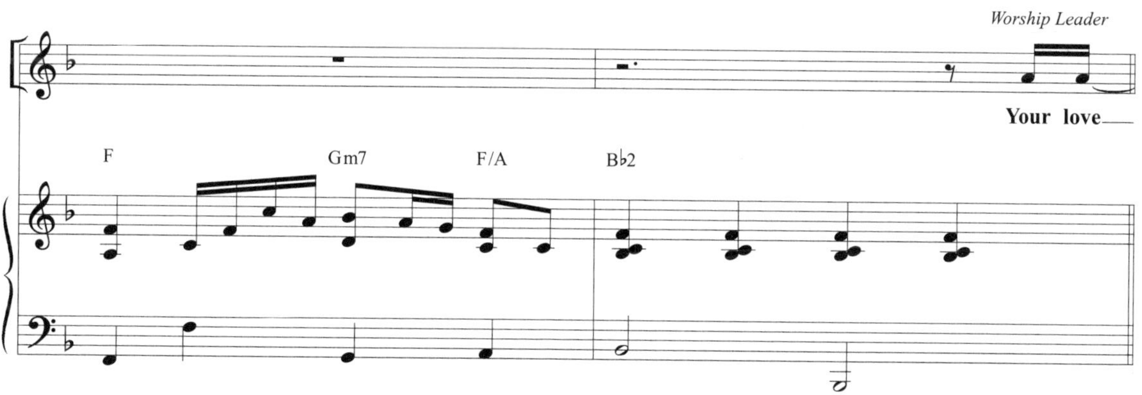

is deep - er than the sea;
Your mer -
F
Gm7
F/A
B♭2
9
cy
nev - er ceas - es to a - maze me;
F
Gm7
F/A
B♭2
Day af - ter day Your love for me re - mains.
Gm7
F/A
B♭2
B♭2/C
1.
All
Your love
F
2.
F

14
VERSE
W.L.
Deep with - in my heart I'm cry - ing out for You;
C/E
Dm
B♭2
Wrap Your arms a - round this heart of mine;
C/E
Dm
C
B♭2
18
Each and ev - 'ry day, Lord, I give You all my praise;
C/E
Dm
B♭2
All
I am fall - ing so in love with You.
Gm7
F/A

22
2, 3.
Your love
Csus
C
F
23
BRIDGE
W.L.
Morn - ing by morn - ing, my eyes can see the sun, and
Praise Team
Morn - ing by morn - ing, Oo,
Dm7
C/E
F
Gm7
F/A
B♭2
all of my wor - ries fade a - way;
all of my wor - ries fade a - way;
Dm7
C/E
F
F/A
B♭

27
Je - sus, my Sav - ior, You are the mu - sic of my heart; You
Je - sus, my Sav - ior, Oo;
Dm7 C/E F Gm7 F/A B♭2
W.L.
gave me the rea - son to give my ver - y best.
Gm7 F/A B♭ E♭ Csus C
32 INSTRUMENTAL
F Gm7 F/A B♭2 F Gm7 F/A
B♭2
36
F Gm7 F/A B♭2

Gm7
F/A
Bb2
Bb2/C
F
40
W.L.
All
Day af - ter day
Your love
for me
re - mains.
Gm7
F/A
Bb2
Bb2/C
F
Gm7
F/A
Bb2
Bb2/C
F
44
W.L.
rit.
Day af - ter day
Your love
for me
re -
Gm7
F/A
Bb2
C2

Medley options: Let The Rain Of Your Presence; O Lord, You're Beautiful.

1277

Surely goodness and mercy shall follow me all the days of my life; And I will dwell in the house of the LORD forever. Psalm 23:6 (NKJ)

Dwell In The House

Words and Music by
MARK MASRI

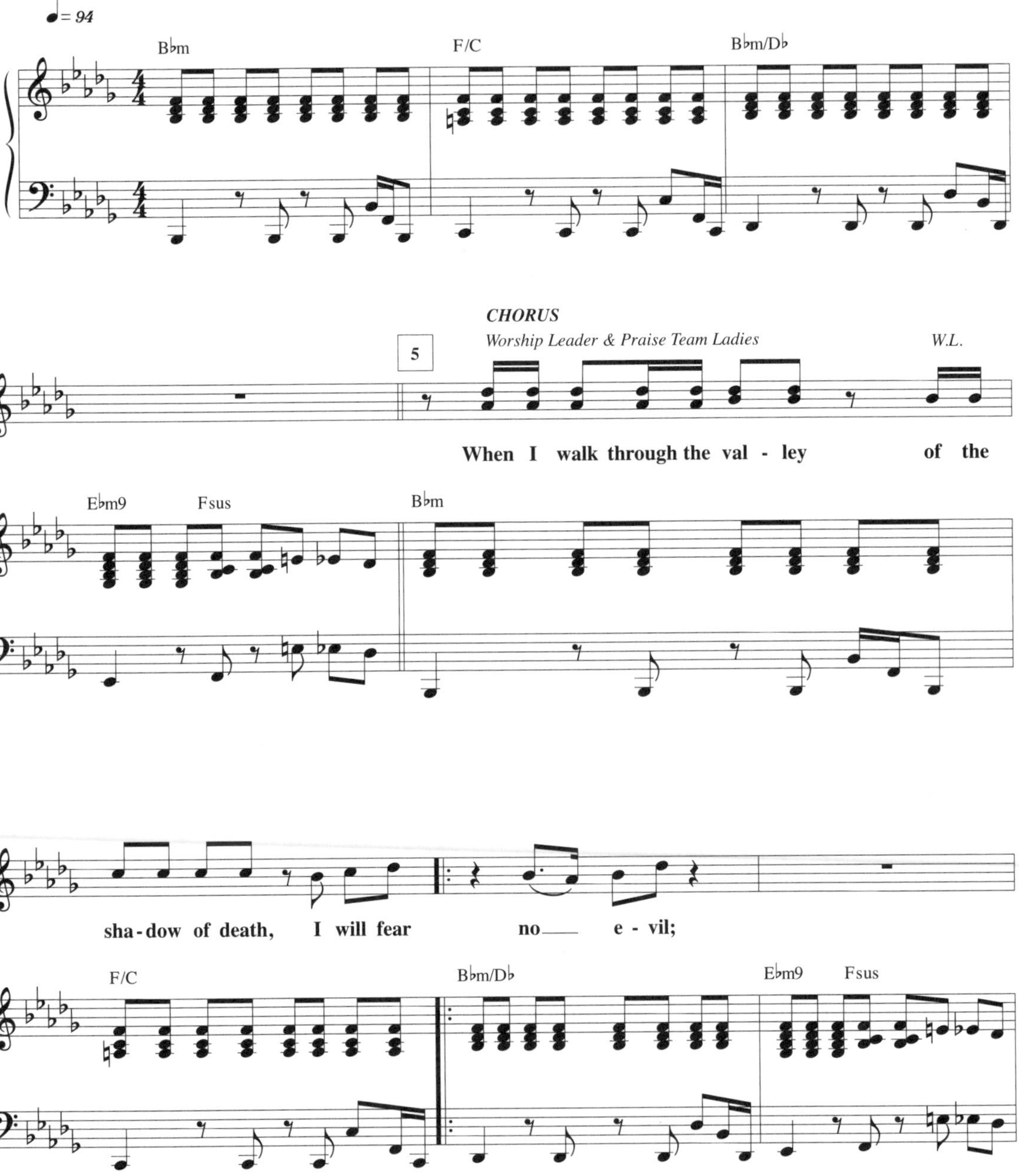
♩= 94
B♭m
F/C
B♭m/D♭
5
CHORUS
Worship Leader & Praise Team Ladies
W.L.
When I walk through the val - ley of the
E♭m9
Fsus
B♭m
sha - dow of death, I will fear no e - vil;
F/C
B♭m/D♭
E♭m9
Fsus

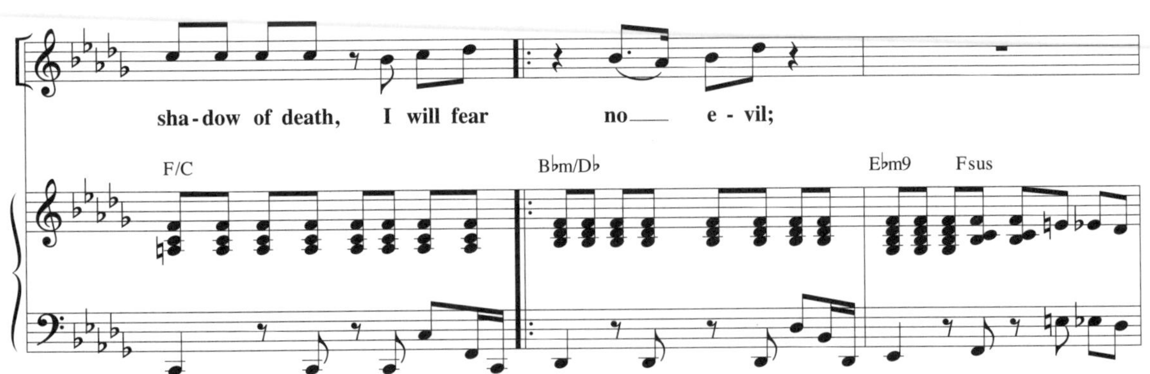

9
Thy rod and Thy staff, they com-fort me all my days,
B♭m
F/C
and all my lone - ly nights;
G♭maj7
E♭m9
Fsus
13
W.L. & P.T. Ladies
Sure-ly good-ness and Your mer - cy
W.L.
will fol-low me all the days
B♭m
F/C
of my life;
All
And I will
17
dwell in the house,
B♭m/D♭
A♭m7
Gaug7
G♭maj7
D♭2/F
A♭

I will dwell in the house, I will
Gbmaj7
Db2/F
Eb2/G
Gbm6
21
dwell in the house of the Lord for-ev-
Db2/F
Eb2/G
Ab
F/A
25
er, and ev - er, and ev - er, and ev -
Praise Team Ladies
For-ev - er, and ev - er, and ev - er.
Bbm
F/C
Bbm/Db

VERSE
27
W.L. 2nd time rubato
er.
1. Sha - dows lurk o - ver my shoul - der,
2. When I feel I've been de - sert - ed, and
E♭m9 Fsus
B♭m
B♭m/A♭
look - ing to en - snare;
no one is a - round,
31
1st time All
2nd time W.L.
I won't ev - er have
I won't ev - er feel
G♭maj7
F7sus
B♭m
to wor - ry, be - cause I'm in Your care.
for - got - ten, be - cause in You I'm found.
1.
B♭m/A♭
E♭m9
F7sus
CHORUS
35
W.L. & P.T. Ladies
When I walk through the val - ley
W.L.
I will fear
B♭m
F/C

2.
A tempo
38
W.L. & P.T. Ladies
W.L.
When I walk through the val - ley of the
F 7sus
Bm
shа - dow of death, I will fear no e - vil;
F♯/C♯
Bm/D
42
Thy rod and Thy staff, they com-fort me all my days,
Em9
F♯sus
Bm
F♯/C♯
and all my lone - ly nights;
Gmaj7
Em9
F♯sus

46
W.L. & P.T. Ladies
Sure-ly good-ness and Your mer-cy will fol-low me all the days
W.L.
Bm
F♯/C♯
of my life;
All
And I will
50
dwell in the house,
Bm/D
Am7
G♯aug7
Gmaj7
D2/F♯
A
I will dwell in the house,
I will
Gmaj7
D2/F♯
E2/G♯
Gm6
54
dwell in the house of the Lord for-ev-
D2/F♯
E2/G♯
A
F♯/A♯

1.
All
58
BRIDGE
Female soloist
er.
I can be safe from harm and dan -
P.T. Ladies
Oo
Bm
E9
Am9
B♭aug7/A♭
D/G
All
W.L.
ger, from things that scare me, be-cause You are al -
F♯
Bm7
E9
Am7
2.
All
ways there; And I will er.
N.C.
Bm

Medley options: Praise Adonai; I Have Kept The Faith.

When the Son of Man comes in His glory, and all the holy angels with Him, then He will sit on the throne of His glory. Matthew 25:31 (NKJ)

Even So

Words and Music by
STEVE MERKEL

Asus A G/B
Cm
A♭/C
B♭sus B♭ Cm
A♭
B♭sus B♭
W.L.
16
VERSE
1. You are wel - come in this place; Be en -
2. We join our hearts to - geth - er; We
Cm
Cm
A♭maj7/C
throned up - on our prais - es; May our wor - ship rise like in - cense as we
come in one ac - cord; The bonds of peace u - nite us in the
B♭sus B♭ Cm
A♭
B♭sus B♭
20
mag - ni - fy the Son, Might - y God of Is - ra - el,
Spir - it of the Lord; You'll clothe us with sal - va - tion in
A♭ B♭ Cm
A♭/C

22
Lamb up-on the throne; All bless - ing and hon - or to our
robes of pur - est white, the bod-y of Mes-si - ah, we are
B♭sus
B♭
Cm
A♭
B♭sus
B♭
All
24
CHORUS
God for-ev-er-more. E - ven so, e-ven so, e-ven
pre-cious in Your sight.
A♭
B♭
Cm
B♭
E♭/G
A♭
E♭/G
28
so, Lord Je-sus, come; All cre-a - tion cries for the re -
B♭
E♭/G
A♭
B♭
Cm
A♭/C
W.L.
turn-ing of our King; Come and take your place on your throne, Je-ru-sa-lem.
E♭/B♭
B♭
Cm
A♭/C
A♭
B♭

1.
2.
W.L.
2. We
Let the
A♭
B♭
Cm
34
BRIDGE
All
Spir - it and the bride say come;
Let the
E♭
to the
Spir - it and the bride say come
38
Li - on and the Lamb;
Heav - en's
King, the great I AM,
come and
A♭/C

take your place on your throne, Je - ru - sa - lem;
P.T. (Oo.)
Cm
Ab/C
Ab
Bb
Ab
Bb

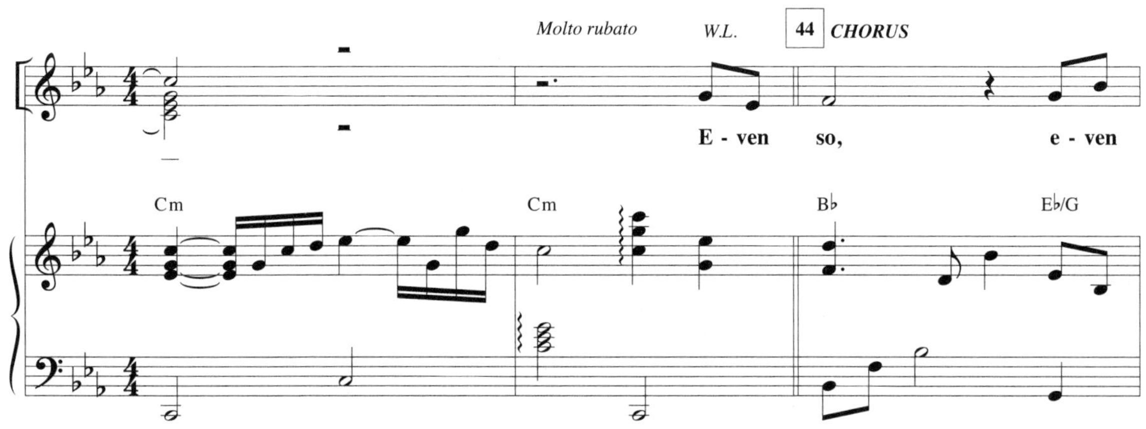
Molto rubato
W.L.
44
CHORUS
E - ven so, e - ven
Cm
Cm
Bb
Eb/G

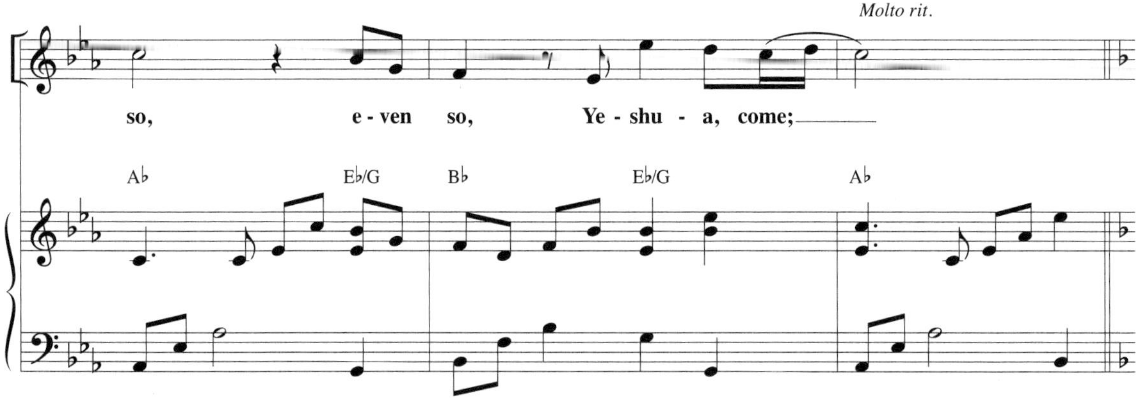
Molto rit.
so, e - ven so, Ye - shu - a, come;
Ab
Eb/G
Bb
Eb/G
Ab

48
A tempo
All
W.L.
All
W.L.
All cre - a - tion cries for the re - turn - ing of our King;
Come and
Dm
B♭/D
F/C
C
take your place on your throne, Je - ru - sa - lem.
All
E - ven
Dm
B♭/D
B♭
C
B♭
C
Dm
52
CHORUS
so, e - ven so, e - ven so, Ye - shu - a,
C
F/A
B♭
F/A
C
F/A
56
come; All cre - a - tion cries for the re -
B♭
C
Dm
B♭/D

Medley options: Let The Weight Of Your Glory Fall; Shalom Jerusalem.

"Holy, holy, holy is the LORD Almighty; the whole earth is full of his glory." Isaiah 6:3 (NIV)

Everything Cries Holy

Words and Music by
ROBIN MARK

17
and His glo - ry fills the heav - ens and the earth;
Glo - ry fills the heav - ens and the earth;
C
F
Am
21
One like a lamb
One like a lamb,
Gsus
G
C
Who was slain is on the throne, so I
slain is on the throne;
Em7
F
C

25
W.L.
cast my crown be - fore You and bow down to pray. For ev' -
Cast my crown be - fore You and bow down to pray.
F
Am
Gsus
G
C
29
CHORUS
ry - thing cries ho - ly, O, ev' - ry - thing cries ho -
Praise Team
Ev - 'ry - thing cries ho - ly, ev - 'ry - thing cries ho -
F
C
Dm7
33
ly, O, ev' - ry - thing cries ho - ly to You, Lord;
ly, ev - 'ry - thing cries ho - ly to You, Lord;
Am7
F
C

37
For ev'ry-thing cries ho-
Ev-'ry-thing cries ho-
Gsus
G
F
ly, O, ev'ry-thing cries ho-ly, O, ev'-
ly, ev-'ry-thing cries ho-ly,
C
Dm7
Am7
41
1, 2.
ry-thing cries ho-ly to You, Lord.
ev-'ry-thing cries ho-ly to You, Lord;
F
C
G

Medley options: Holy Lamb Of God; We Shall Behold Him.

We live by faith, not by sight. 2 CORINTHIANS 5:7 (NIV)

Faith In You

Words and Music by
LINDELL COOLEY and LENNY LeBLANC

1st time W.L.
13
me; I put my faith in You, no mat-ter where
All
F
C
G
the road may lead me;
Am
G
F
17
W.L.
You are my Sav - ior,
P.T. Oo;
C/G
my clos-est friend,
All
One touch from You and I'm whole a-gain;
W.L.
I put my faith,
E7/G♯
Am
G
F
21
Praise Team
I put my faith
1, 2.
All
in You.
C/G
G 7sus
C

27
VERSE
W.L.
1. When the sha - dows hide the truth, Your love shines through,
2. When I look in - to my heart and there is no song,
F
C
F
31
with a voice that beck - ons me to fol -
e - ven in my weak - est hour You make
C
F
C
35
low You;
me strong;
When I sail in - to
Lord, You are my on -
Gsus
G
F
a storm or some - how go a - stray,
ly hope, my guid - ing star,
C
F
C

37
You're the One Who is al - ways there to light the way.
and I will al-ways find a place where You are.
F
C
Gsus
C/G
3.
I put my faith in You.
I put my faith
G
G7sus
C
44
CHORUS
in You,
You are the One Who will nev - er leave
C
G
Am
G
48
me; I put my faith in You, no mat-ter where
F
C
G

52
W.L.
You are my Sav - ior,
the road may lead me;
P.T. Oo;
Am
G
F
C/G
my clos-est friend,
All
W.L.
One touch from You and I'm whole a-gain; I put my faith,
E7/G♯
Am
G
F
56
P.T.
W.L.
P.T.
I put my faith,
I put my faith,
I put my faith
C/G
G/F
C/E
W.L. ad libs
60
P.T.
I put my faith,
F
C/G
G/F

Medley options: The Name Of Jesus; Ancient Of Days.

Give thanks to the LORD, for he is good; his love endures forever. I Chronicles 16;34 (NIV)

Forever

Words and Music by
CHRIS TOMLIN

13
VERSE
All
1st time Melody only
thanks to the Lord, our God and King, His love endures for-ev-
might-y hand and out-stretched arm, His love endures for-ev-
ris-ing to the set-ting sun, His love endures for-ev-
G
W.L.
17
All
er; He is good, He is a-bove all things, His
er; For the life that has been re-born, His
er; By the grace of God we will car-ry on; His
C2
Men
21
Sing praise,
love en-dures for-ev-er; Sing praise,
love en-dures for-ev-er;
love en-dures for-ev-er;
Ladies
praise,
G
D

sing praise.
Sing
Sing
praise;
C2/E
25
praise,
sing praise.
praise;
praise,
D
C2/E
1.
W.L.
2. His
2, 3.
All
For - ev -
C2/E

30
CHORUS
er God is faith - ful, for-ev - er God is strong;
G
Em7
34
CHORUS
For-ev - er God is with us, for-ev -
G/D
38
er;
For-ev - er God is faith -
C2
G
ful, for-ev - er God is strong; For-ev -
Em7

42
er God is with us, for - ev - er,
G/D
C2
45
1.
G5
49
W.L.
3. From the
G5
2.
G5
Em7
54
G/D

56
All
His
C2
58
BRIDGE
1st time Melody only
love en - dures for - ev - er,
His love en - dures for - ev -
G
Em7
62
1, 2.
er,
His love en - dures for - ev - er,
for - ev -
G/D
3.
er.
His
er,
for - ev -
C2

67
er.
For - ev -
C2
70 CHORUS
er God is faith - ful,
for - ev - er God is strong;
A
F♯m7
74
For - ev - er God is with us,
for - ev -
A/E
78
er;
For - ev - er God is faith -
D2
A

Medley options: Only A God Like You; We Rejoice In You.

Let them give glory to the LORD and proclaim his praise... Isaiah 42:12 (NIV)

Give Us The Sounds

Words and Music by
TOMMY WALKER

move Your heart, that ush - er in Your Spir-it's pow'r.
will fear; They will put their trust in the liv - ing God.
E5
13
CHORUS
All
Glo - ry, glo - ry, glo - ry to the Lamb of God;
D2
A
Esus
E
17
Glo - ry, glo - ry, glo - ry to the
D2
A
Lamb of God.
21
Esus
E

1.
W.L.
2. He's
2.
INSTRUMENTAL
E5
E5
E5
E5
Repeat twice
32
BRIDGE
All
Glo - o, o -
E
F♯m/E

36
o,
o
ri - a,
we
E
B/E
40
give
You
all
the
glo
ry, Lord;
E
F♯m/B
E/G♯
F♯m/A
E/B
B
44
Glo
o,
C♯m7
A/C♯
C♯m7
F♯m/C♯
C♯m7
A/C♯
48
o
o,
o
G♯m/D♯
D♯m7
G♯m/D♯
B/D♯
E
F♯m/A
E/A
B/A
A

52
ri - a, we give You all the
B B/A E/G♯ F♯m/A E/B A/C♯
56
glo - ry, Lord.
E/B B E A2 E
60 VERSE W.L.
1. Give us the sounds of praise,
A2 E
O God, the sounds that bring Your glo - ry down;

64
Give us the rhy-thms that move Your heart, that ush-er in Your
E
68
CHORUS
W.L.
P.T.
Spir-it's pow'r. Glo-ry, glo-ry,
D2
W.L.
P.T.
W.L.
72
P.T.
glo-ry, glo-ry, to the Lamb of God, to the
A2
A
A/E
E
W.L.
76
P.T.
Lamb of God; We're sing-ing glo-ry, glo-ry,
F♯m/E
E
D2

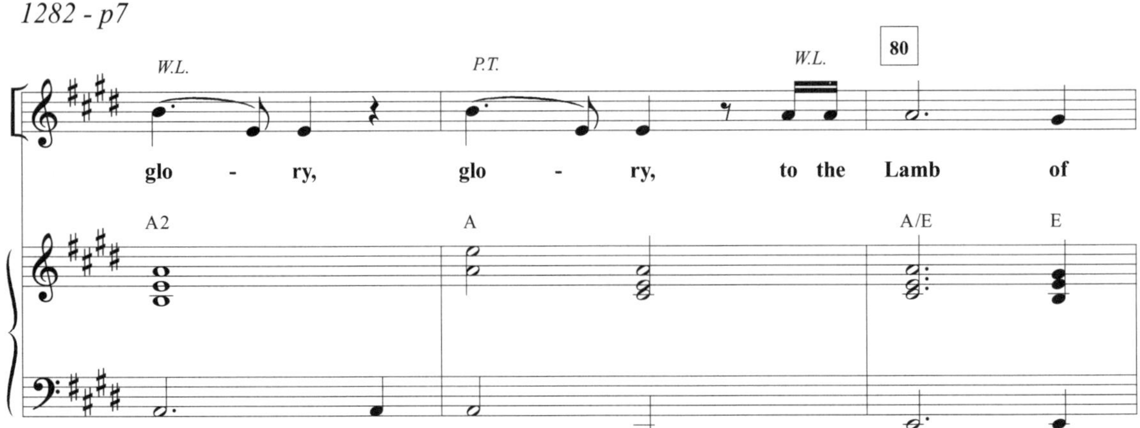

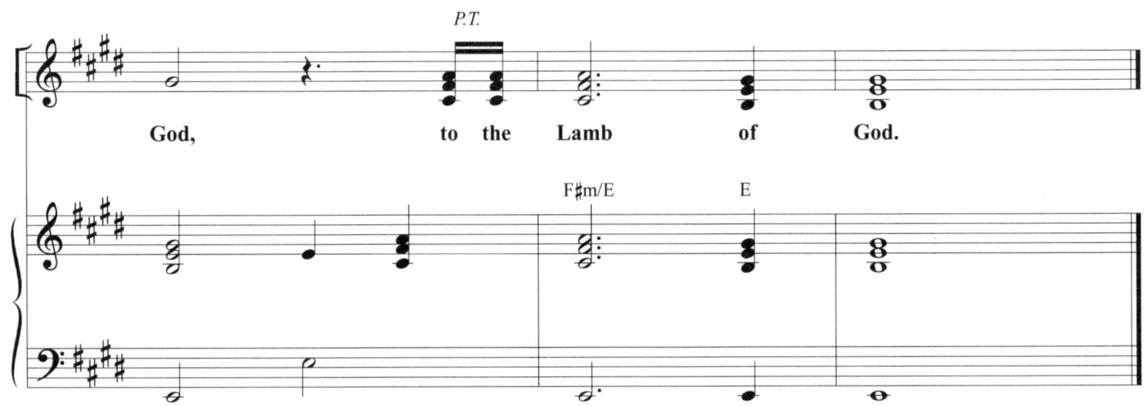

Medley options: My Redeemer Lives (MORGAN); Jesus, That Name.

...Give glory to the Lord, the God of Israel, and give Him the praise... Joshua 7:19 (NIV)

Glory To The Lord

Words and Music by
LYNN DESHAZO

Who made the stars by the Word of His pow - er?
Who is the way in this mar - vel - ous hour?
A
E
G♯sus
G♯
15
All
Who put the spir - it in man,
Who stirs the heart of a man
and caus - es all the earth
and caus - es all His saints
C♯m
B
A
1st time melody only
to cry out glo - ry?
to cry out glo - ry?
Glo - ry to the
E
G♯sus
G♯
21
CHORUS
Lord, wor - ship Him, the God of our sal - va -
C♯m
B
A
E

25
tion; Glo-ry to the Lord, hon - or Him, He reigns,
B
C♯m
B A
29
He rules the na - tions; He is right - eous and wor -
E
B
F♯m7
thy to be wor-shipped and a - dored; Lift your
C♯m
B
Amaj7
G♯m7
33
1.
voic - es and give glo-ry to the Lord.
F♯m7
G♯sus G♯
C♯m
B A

37
C♯m
B
A
3
2.
39
Instrumental
Lord.
C♯m
B
A
E
B
43
F♯m
C♯m
B
A2
G♯m
47
F♯m

49
Glo-ry to the
G♯sus G♯
A
F/A
B♭
C2
51
CHORUS
Lord, wor - ship Him, the God of our sal - va -
Dm
C
B♭
F
55
tion; Glo-ry to the Lord, hon - or Him, He reigns,
C
Dm
C
B♭
59
He rules the na - tions; He is right - eous and wor -
F
C
Gm7

thy to be wor-shipped and a - dored; Lift your
Dm C B♭maj7 Am7
63
voic - es and give glo - ry to the
Gm7 Asus A
1.
2.
glo - ry to the Lord, glo - ry to the
Asus A Dm C B♭
66
Lord, glo - ry to the Lord.
Dm C B♭ Dm C B♭
70

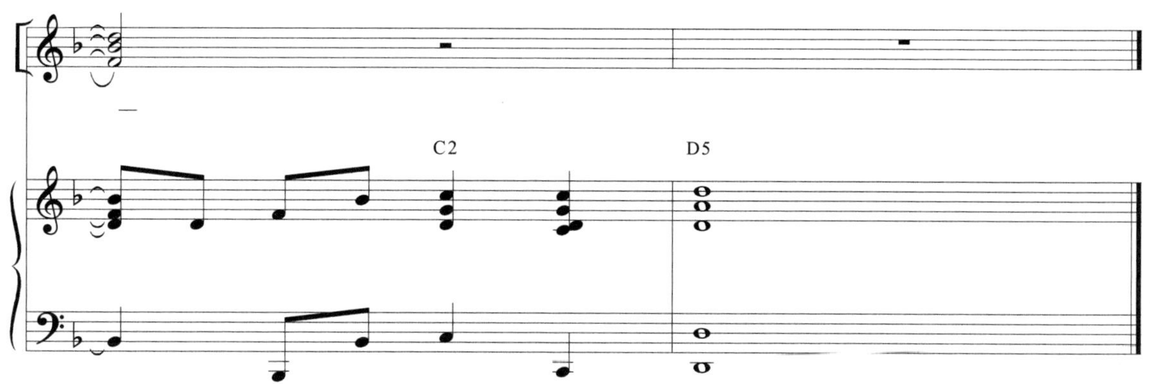

Medley options: O Deliverer; One God.

1284

Lift up your heads, O you gates; be lifted up, you ancient doors, that the King of glory may come in. Psalm 24:7 (NIV)

Glory To The Lord Our God

Words and Music by
STEVE MERKEL

13
2
in; Be lift - ed up, O an - cient doors; Let the King
G C F G Am
of Glo - ry come in;
1.
2.
in. The
W.L.
F G C C
18
VERSE
al - tars we've built and the works we have done can nev - er com - pare to the
Praise Team
Oo; Oo;
G C F G G C

2
22
Sav - ior's love; The hearts of the hum - ble are tem - ples of
Oo, tem - ples of
F G C F
25
praise as we wor - ship the An - cient of Days, as we
praise; wor - ship the An - cient of Days, as we
C G Am F
wor - ship the An - cient of Days.
wor - ship the An - cient of Days.
C G C

29
BRIDGE
All
Glo - ry to the Lord, our God; Glo - ry to the
G F C F C
33
Lamb on the throne; We o - pen wide the gates of our hearts, with our
Am G G F C
37
lips we rise up and praise as we wor - ship the An - cient of
Am F G F G
1.
Days.
C F G C F C

G
42
C
F
G
Am

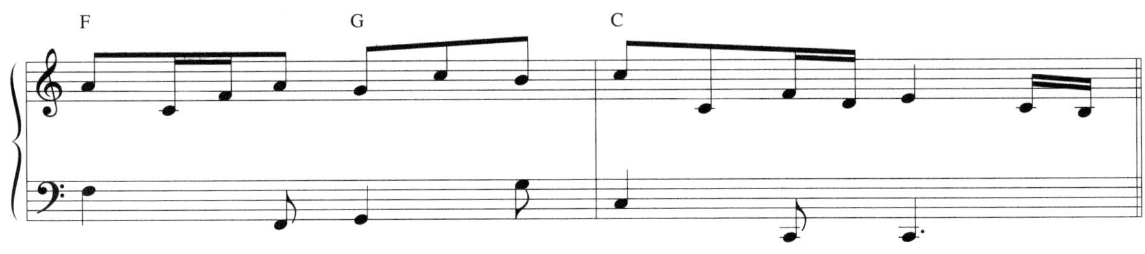
F
G
C

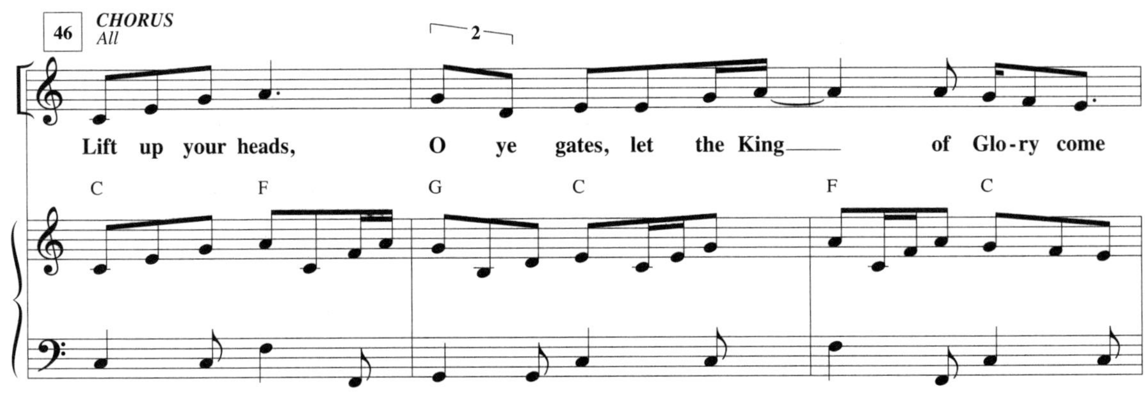
46
CHORUS
All
2
Lift up your heads, O ye gates, let the King of Glo-ry come
C
F
G
C
F
C

50
2
in; Be lift-ed up, O an - cient doors; Let the King
G
C
F
G
Am

54
VERSE
W.L.
of Glo-ry come in.
Who can as-cend to the hill
P.T.
Oo;
F G C G C
of the Lord,
peo-ple of clean hearts and hands;
Oo;
F G C F
58
You, who are right-eous and seek-ing His face, come and
Oo, seek-ing His face;
G C F F

61
wor - ship the An - cient of Days, come and wor - ship the An - cient of
wor - ship the An - cient of Days, come and wor - ship the An - cient of
C G Am F C G
Days.
Days.
C
2.
D.S.
Days.
C
67
3.
Days.
C F G C F C G

71
Am
F
G
C
Dm
C/E
F
G
75
F/A
G/B
2
F2
C/F
G
C5
2
81
CHORUS
All
Lift up your heads,
C5
C
F/C
2
O ye gates, let the King of Glo - ry come
G/C
C
F/C
C

Medley options: Your Throne, O God; Great Is The Lord (SMITH).

She opens her arms to the poor and extends her hands to the needy. Prov. 31:20 (NIV)

Grandma's Hands

Words and Music by
BILL WITHERS

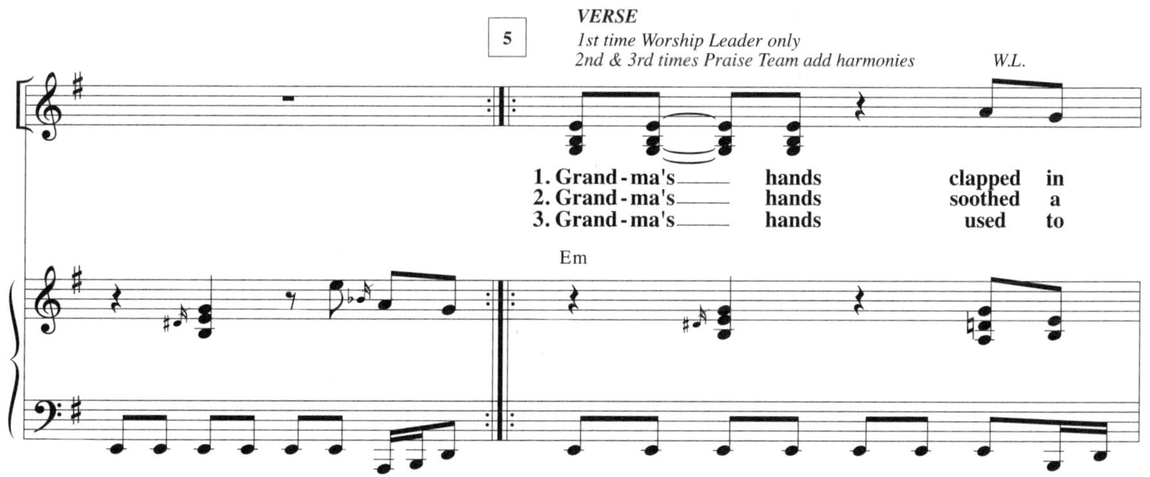

9
2nd & 3rd times Praise Team add harmonies
W.L.
bou - rine so well. Grand - ma's hands used to
some - times and swell. Grand - ma's hands used to
each time I'd fall. Grand - ma's hands Lord, they
Em
is - sue out a warn - ing, She'd say,
lift a face and tell her, She'd say,
real - ly came in hand - y, She'd say,
1, 2.
Ron - ny, don't you run so fast,
Ba - by, Grand - ma un - der - stands,
B7
A7
you might fall on a piece of glass;
that you real - ly love that man;
B7
A7

13
2nd & 3rd times P.T. add harmonies
There might be snakes there in that grass; Grand-ma's hands.
Put your faith in Je-sus' hands; Grand-ma's hands.
B7
A7
Em
3.
W.L.
E-dith, don't you whip that boy;
B7
A7
17
What you want to spank him for? He did-n't steal that can-dy from no store. But I
B7
A7
B7
A7
don't have Grand-ma an-y-more. When I get to Hea-ven, I'm gon-na look for
B7
A7
B7
A7

Oo;
Em
Em
Yeah.
Em

For great is the LORD and most worthy of praise.... Psalm 96:4 (NIV)

Great Is He

Words and Music by
AUTHOR UNKNOWN

1286 - p2
9
CHORUS
Praise Team Sopranos
Hal - le - lu - jah, hal - le - lu - jah, hal - le -
C C/E F G E7/G♯
lu - jah, He is won - der - ful.
Am7 Dm7 G 7sus G C
13
CHORUS
Praise Team Men
Hal - le - lu - jah, sal - va - tion and glo - ry,
C C/E F G E7/G♯
hon - or and pow - er, He is won - der - ful.
Am7 Dm7 G 7sus G C

Medley options: There Is A Fountain Filled With Blood; Anointing Fall On Me.

1287

..."Hallelujah! For our Lord God Almighty reigns." Revelation 19:6 (NIV)

Hallelujah

Words and Music by
CRAIG SMITH

9
W.L.
3
Your eyes blaze like fire (re), crowns up - on Your head,
King of the A - ges, Bright and Morn - ing Star,
F C/E F C/E
1st time W.L. only, lower note
2nd time add P.T. Men, upper note
All (Melody top note)
You are the Word of God, the Be - gin - ning the End. Hal - le -
Won - der - ful Coun - se - lor, all of life is Your charge.
F C/E Gsus G C/E
13 CHORUS
lu - jah, our Lord Al - might - y reigns; Je - sus
F C/E F C/E
Christ our Sav - ior reigns; Hal - le -
F C/E Gsus G C/E

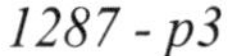

17

lu - jah, our Lord Al - might - y reigns, our

F C/E F C/E

1. 2, 3. *Last time D.S.*

Lord, our King, our God. Hal - le -

F C/E Gsus G Gsus G C/E

4.

Gsus G Gsus G G

Medley options: No Other Name.

I desire to do your will, O my God... Psalm 40:8 (NIV)

Have Your Way

Words and Music by
CLAIRE CLONINGER and DON MOEN

Tenors add harmony
and have Your way;
As we wait,
D
G D/G C/G G
10
as we pray,
Both times, female soloist
We wait on You;
We pray to You;
Am7
D
G D/F♯
14
Speak Your Word
in - to our hearts,
Em7
Am7

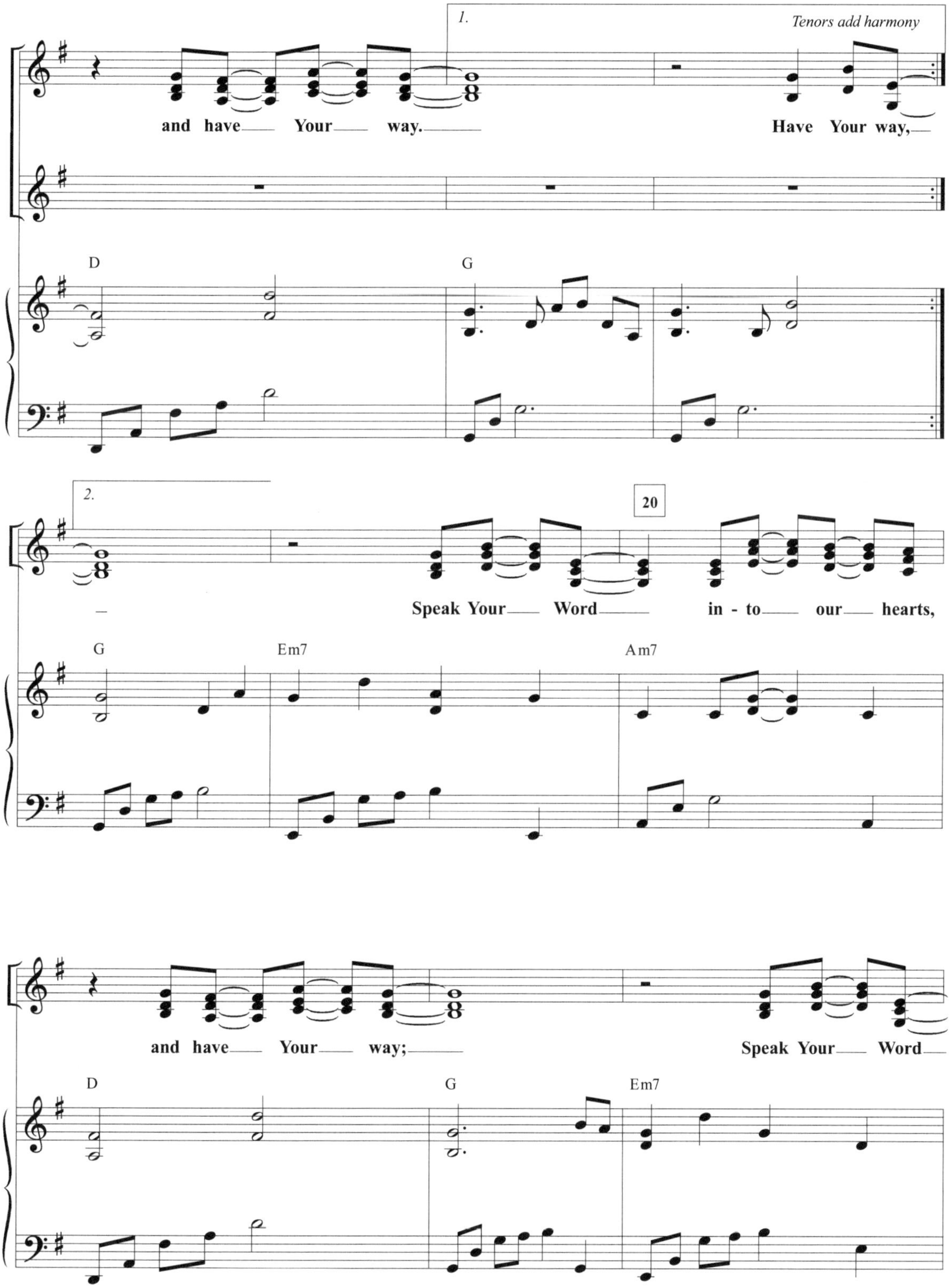

1.

Tenors add harmony

and have Your way. Have Your way,

D G

2.

20

Speak Your Word in - to our hearts,

G Em7 Am7

Medley options: Here We Are (CLONINGER/MOEN); More of You (MERKEL).

..."Fear not, for I have redeemed you; I have summoned you by name; you are mine. Isaiah 43:1 (NIV)

He Knows My Name

Words and Music by
TOMMY WALKER

CHORUS
1st time W.L.
2nd & 3rd time All
10
He knows my name, He knows my ev - 'ry thought;
Bb F C 7sus Eb/F F 7/A Bb F
14
He sees each tear that falls, and
C F Bb F C Dm7
hears me when I call.
Bb C C 7sus F C/F Bb/F F Eb/F F
2.
D.S.
3.
Rubato
20
CHORUS
W.L.
And He knows your name;
F Bb F C Fsus F

Medley options: How Could I But Love You; You Are My All In All.

...That the name of our Lord Jesus Christ may be glorified in you, and you in Him...2 Thessalonians 1:12 (NKJ)

He Saved Us To Show His Glory

Words and Music by
TOMMY WALKER

P.T.
me? So you could be His child for - giv - en;
C2 Dsus G/B C2 Dsus
13
W.L.
Why did He save you?
P.T.
So
G Dsus Em7 C2 Dsus
we could show His grace and mer - cy;
17
W.L.
Why did He save
G/B C2 Dsus G Dsus Em7
P.T.
me? To take His glo - ry to the na - tions.
C2 Dsus G/B C2 Dsus

21
VERSE
All
1. Set a - part to de - clare His glor - ious praise,
2. Set a - part to pro - claim the glor - ious news
Em7
D
Am/C
25
Parts 2nd time only
cho - sen to ra - di - ate His glo -
that all is for - giv - en now, the old
G/B
Em7
A/C♯
ry and His grace;
can be made new;
29
Once with - out hope, His
Once with - out hope, His
Em/D
D
D 7sus
D
Em7
D
mer - cy we've re - ceived,
mer - cy we've re - ceived,
33
so let's show the world what it means
so let's show the world what it means
Am/C
G/B
Em7
A/C♯

1.
2.
to be re - deemed.
to be re - deemed.
Em/D
D
38
G
Fsus/C
42 INSTRUMENTAL
B♭2/D
B♭/E♭
Fsus
Gsus/A
46
G/B
C2
1.
2.
W.L.
He
Dsus
Fsus/C

BRIDGE
1st time W.L. only
2nd time All melody
3rd & 4th times All parts
51
saved us to show His glo - ry, He saved us to show
G Dsus Em7 C2 Dsus G/B C2
His love; He saved us to show His glo - ry and
55
Dsus G Dsus Em7 C2 Dsus
His love.
1, 2, 3.
All
He
G/B C2 Dsus
4.
Dsus
60
G

Medley options: Rise Up And Praise Him; Jesus, We Celebrate Your Victory.

1291

...Let us offer the sacrifice of praise to God...giving thanks to His name. Hebrews 13:15 (KJV)

Here We Are

Words and Music by
CLAIRE CLONINGER and DON MOEN

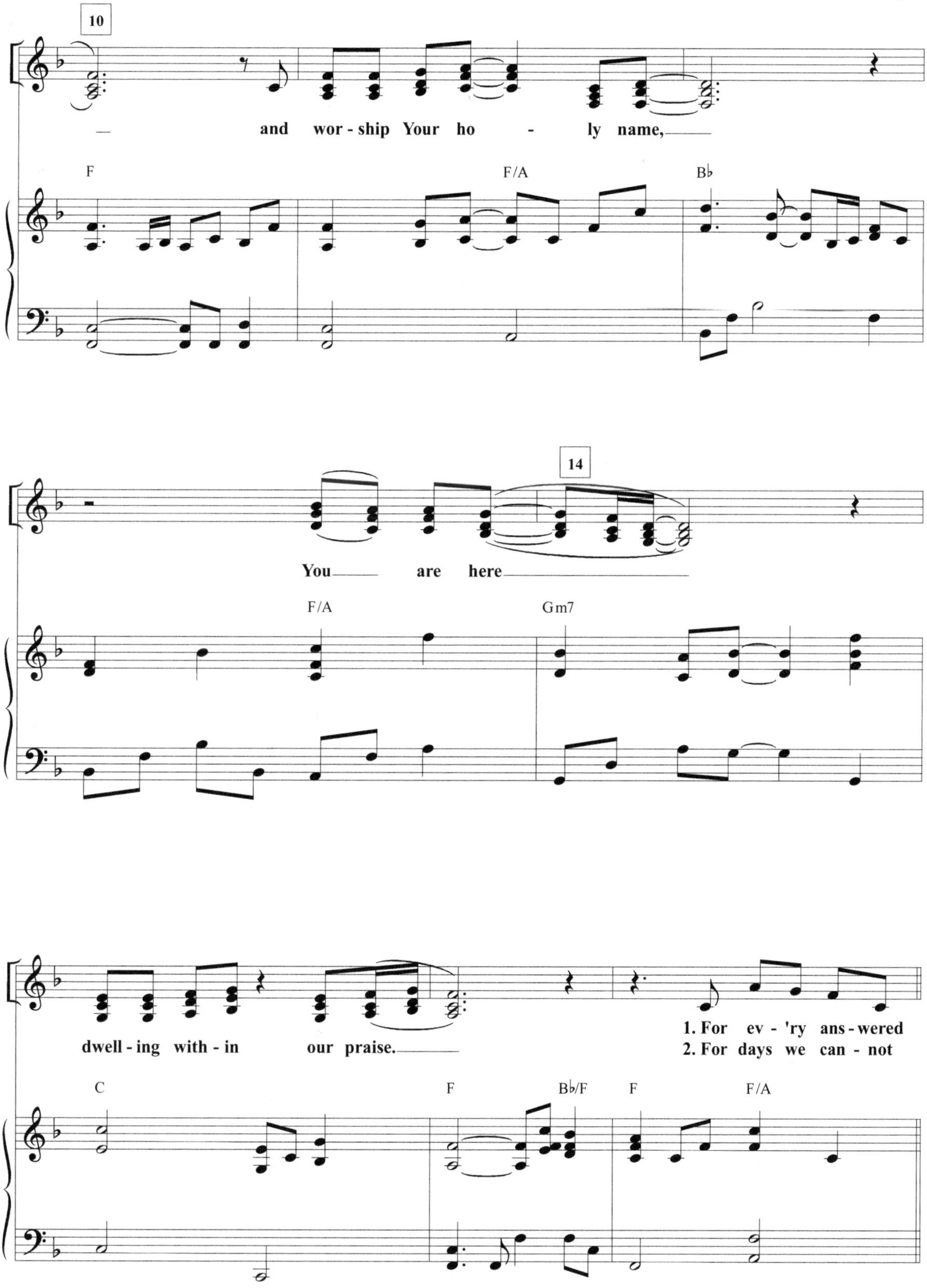
10
and wor - ship Your ho - ly name,
F
F/A
B♭
14
You are here
F/A
Gm7
dwell - ing with - in our praise.
1. For ev - 'ry ans - wered
2. For days we can - not
C
F
B♭/F
F
F/A

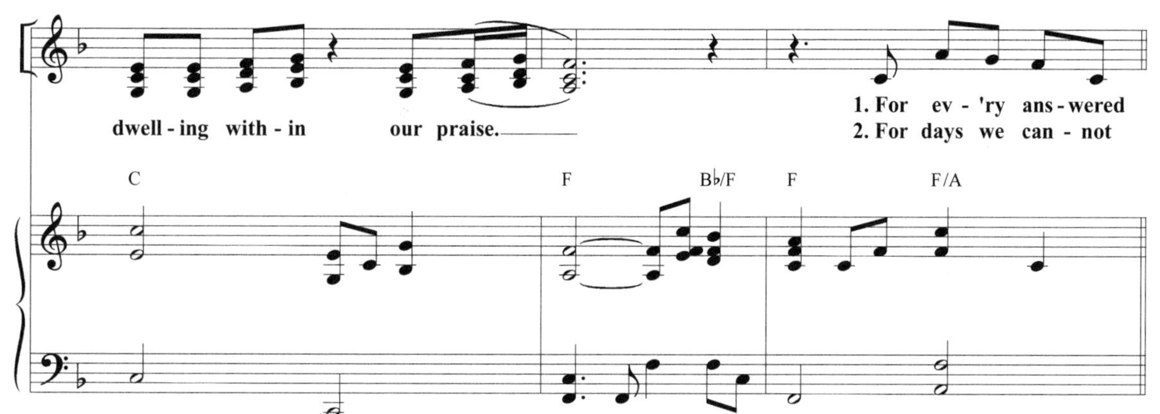

18 VERSE

pray'r, for al-ways be-ing there,
see, for all that's yet to be,

2nd time, female soloist

For days we can-not see; So much is yet to be;

Bb C F

22

for love that hears us when we call, for arms that lift us
the tri-als we may have to face, when we'll be lean-ing

Eb/Bb Bb C

26

when we fall, You have al-ways been right be-
on Your grace, it will be Your strength that saves

P.T. Ladies both times

Oo;

Gm/F F Em7(b5) A7 Dm

3
side us, lead - ing us all a - long the way, and we've made
- us, Your love that makes us strong, and through
Oo;
Dm/C
B♭
F/A
30
it through, be - cause of You.
it all, we'll sing this song.
1. Made it through,
2. Through it all,
Gm7
Fsus/C
1.
All
And here we are,
2.
ritard
Here we are,
ritard
C
C/D
D
C/D
D

35

lift - ing our hands to You;

a tempo

G G/B C

39

Here we are, giv - ing You thanks for

G/B Am D

all You do; And as we praise

43

and

C/G G C/D D C/D G C/G

wor - ship Your ho - ly name, You are here

G G/B C G/B

Medley options: Praise to You; Praise to the Lord.

1292

For great is your love, reaching to the heavens; your faithfulness reaches to the skies. Psalm 57:10 (NIV)

How Could I But Love You

Words and Music by
TOMMY WALKER

serve You, when on the cross You were the ser - vant of all;
E/A
F♯m/A
F♯/A♯
Bsus
B
13
How could I but fol - low You, when all Your ways lead to free-dom and life;
E/A
E/G♯
C♯m
17
How could I but love You, my
A
E
E/A
F♯m/A
20
Sav - ior and my God
Bsus
B
E
E/A
F♯m/A

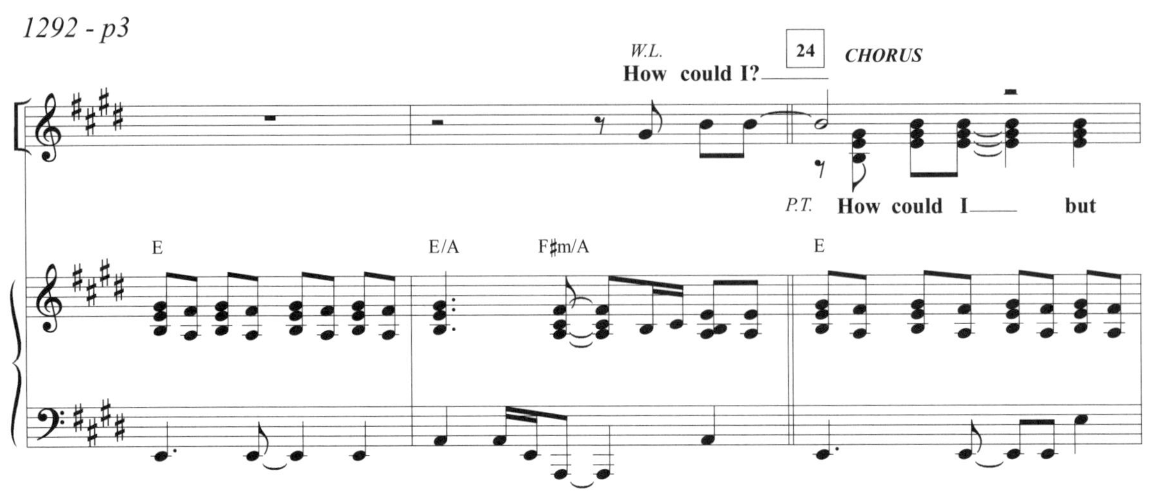
W.L.
How could I?
24
CHORUS
P.T.
How could I but
E
E/A
F#m/A
E

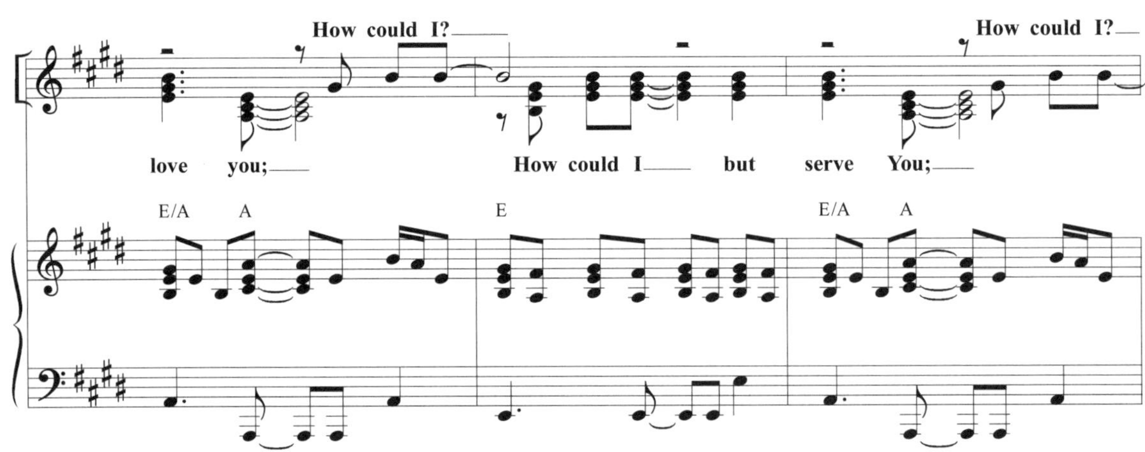
How could I?
How could I?
love you;
How could I but serve You;
E/A
A
E
E/A
A

28
How could I but fol - low You, my God.
E
E/A
A
E

32
VERSE
All
How could I but love You, my
E/A
A
F
F/B♭
Gm/B♭
Com - fort - er, my Strength;
36
How could I but
C 7sus
C
F
C/F
B♭/F
F
serve You, when in this life You've been so faith - ful and true;
F/B♭
Gm/B♭
G/B
Csus C
Csus C
40
How could I but fol - low You, when some-day soon You'll o - pen Heav-en for me;
F/B♭
B♭
F/A
Dm

44
How could I but love You, my
B♭
F
F/B♭
Gm/B♭
47
Sav - ior and my God.
Csus
C
F
F/B♭
Gm/B♭
W.L. How could I?
F
F/B♭
Gm/B♭
51
CHORUS
How could I?
P.T. How could I but love you;
F
F/B♭
B♭

Medley options: Let The Peace Of God Reign; Be Magnified.

1293

How good and pleasant it is when brothers live together in unity! Psalm 133:1 (NIV)

How Good And Pleasant

Words and Music by
TOMMY WALKER

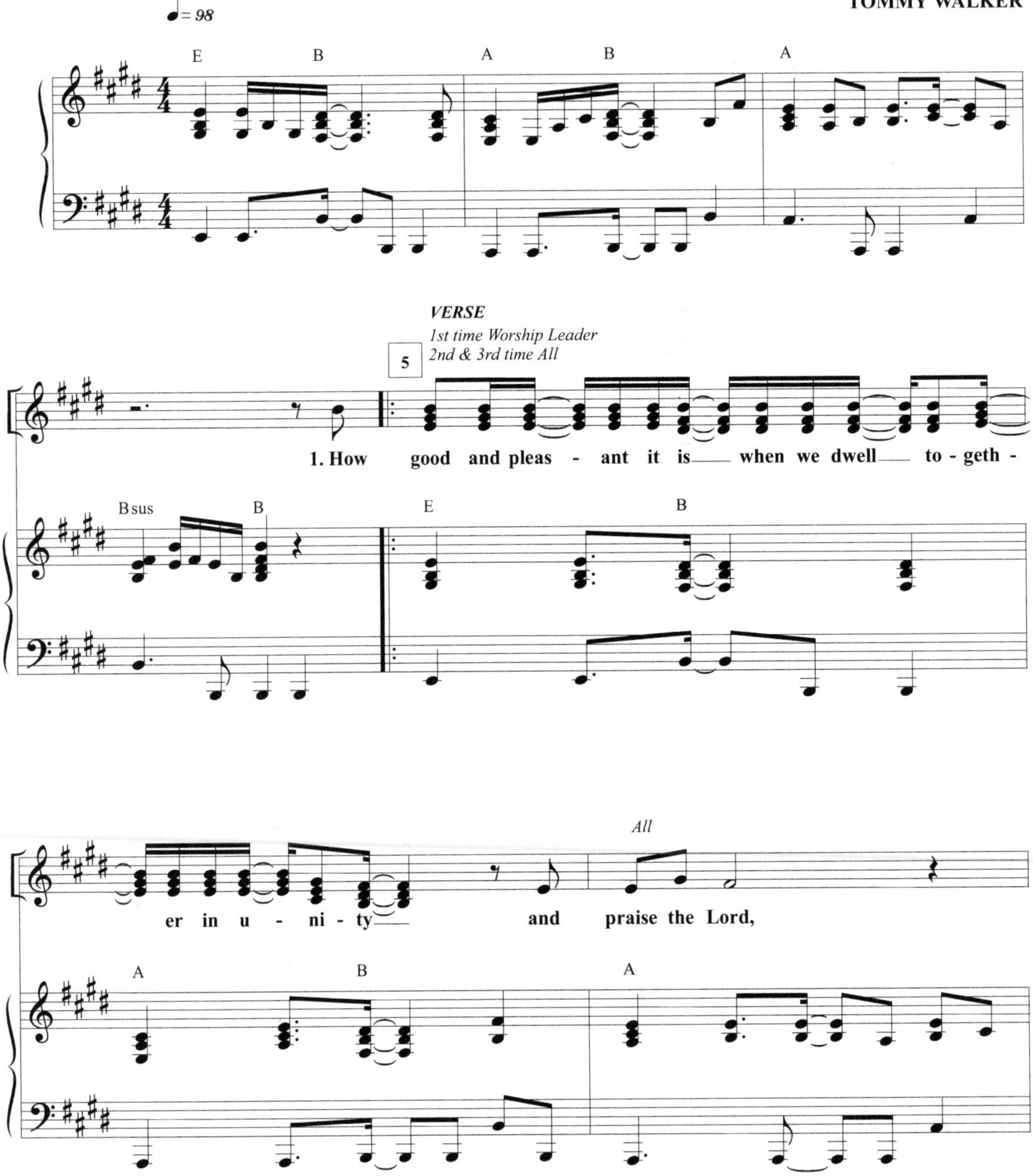
♩= 98
E
B
A
B
A
VERSE
1st time Worship Leader
2nd & 3rd time All
5
1. How good and pleas - ant it is when we dwell to - geth -
Bsus
B
E
B
er in u - ni - ty
and praise the Lord,
All
A
B
A

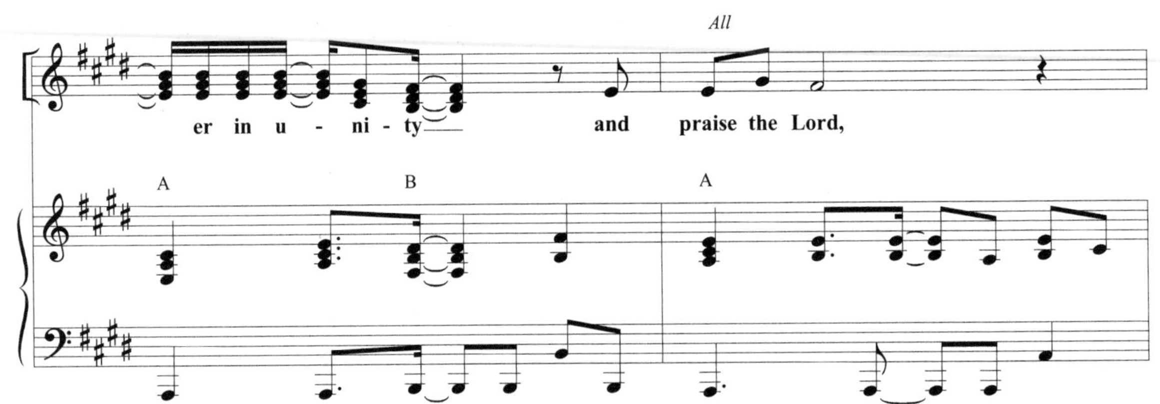

1st time W.L.
9
2nd & 3rd time All
praise the Lord; How good and pleas - ant it is when we dwell to-geth -
Bsus
E
B
er in u - ni-ty, and praise the Lord, praise the Lord. Praise the
All
A
B
A
Bsus
13
CHORUS
Lord, praise the
E
B
A
Lord; Praise the
E
B
A

17
Lord,
praise the
E
B
A
last time to Coda
1.
All
Lord.
How
E
B
A
2.
22
A2
E
B
A
B
3.
How
A
Bsus
A2

27
BRIDGE
All
Show - ers of bless - ing, show - ers they fall,
A
E2/G♯
F♯m7
31
when we love and live in u - ni - ty, when we
Bsus
B
D
D/G
G
lift one voice, loud and strong.
F♯m7
A/B
B
36
INSTRUMENTAL
E
B
A
E
B

Sing 2nd time
W.L.

40 VERSE

2. As far as the east __ is to __ the west, the north __ __ is to the south, What we're gon - na do,

P.T.
praise the Lord, praise the Lord;

W.L.
From the

44
ris - ing of __ the sun, __ to the go - in' down of the same, __ We're all __ gon - na

P.T.
praise the Lord,

A E B A B A Bsus E B A B A

W.L.
3
48
praise the Lord; No mat - ter who comes a - gainst us, no
Bsus
E
B
mat - ter what the world says, We're gon - na praise the Lord,
P.T.
A
B
A
W.L.
52
praise the Lord; 'Cause we know it won't be long we'll see our Sav -
Bsus
E
B
ior com - ing in those clouds, We're all gon - na
A
B

P.T.
praise the Lord,
praise the Lord.
D.S. al Coda
All
Praise the
A
Bsus
Coda
57
CHORUS
Praise the
Lord,
praise the
A
E
B
A
Lord;
Praise the
E
B
A
61
Lord,
praise the
E
B
A

Medley options: Speak To One Another; I Will Celebrate (BALOCHE).

Let us fix our eyes on Jesus, the author and perfecter of our faith... Hebrews 12:2 (NIV)

I Fix My Eyes On You

Words and Music by
TOMMY WALKER and BOB WILSON

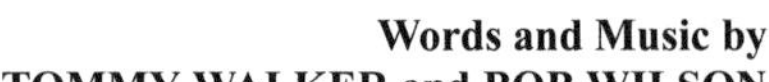

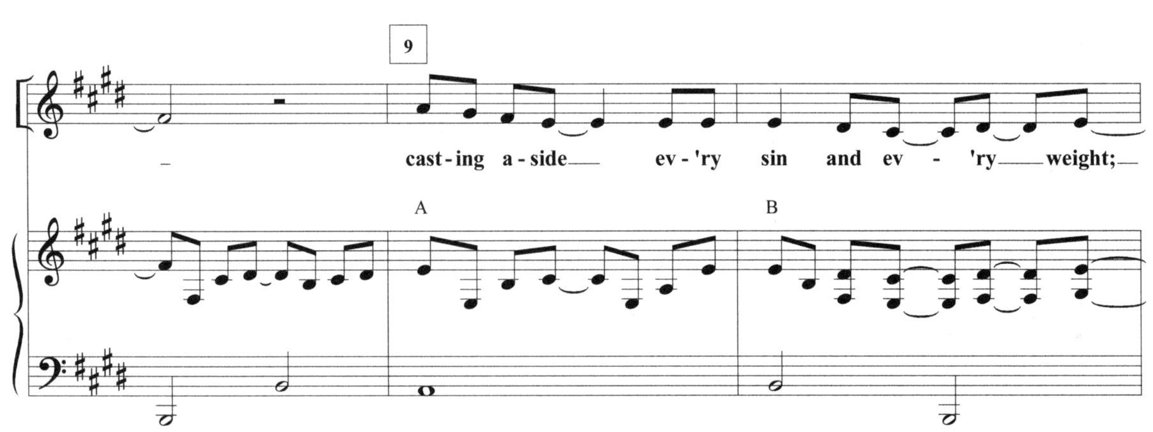

13
I fix my eyes on You, I
E
B 7sus
E2
17
lay my bur - dens down,
let - ting the cares of this
B
A
world now fade a - way.
B
E
21
CHORUS
1st time W.L. only
2nd & 3rd time All
One thing I ask, this one thing
E/A
B/D♯
A/E
E

25
I seek, that I may dwell in Your house, O Lord, my King;
G♯m7 C♯m
E/A
B/D♯
29
1st time W.L. and Duet vocalist (middle note)
2nd & 3rd time All
All the days of my life,
E
F♯m7 E/G♯
E/A
I want to gaze up - on Your beau - ty and
B/D♯
A/E E
G♯m7 C♯m7
33
last time to Coda
1.
seek You in this ho - ly place.
A
B
E

37
B/D♯
All
2.
D.S. al Coda
I
A
Bsus
B
E
F♯m7
E/G♯
Coda
45
All
2nd time melody
All the days of my life,
E
E/A
I want to gaze up - on Your beau - ty and
B/D♯
A/E
E
G♯m7
C♯m7

Medley options: More Than Anything (CHRISTENSEN); O Lord, You're Beautiful.

I seek you with all my heart.... PSALM 119:10 (NIV)

I Give My Heart To You

Words and Music by
LINDELL COOLEY and LENNY LeBLANC

13
All the dreams that I've been chas - ing
Just one mo - ment in Your pre - sence
F
Gm7
B♭2
C2
C
17
dis - ap - pear when I see Your face.
I could leave this world be - hind
Gm7
B♭2
C
All
I
21
CHORUS
believe You are the One
F
Dm7
Am7

25
Who gave
Your-self
for me,
B♭
F
Dm7
29
and so
I pledge
B♭2
C
F
Add parts last time
my love
so true;
For - ev -
Dm7
Am7
B♭
33
er,
and
ev
-
er
B♭
C
Gm7

37
last time to Coda
I give my heart to You.
Dm7
B♭
C

1.
41
B♭2
C
Dm9

2.
B♭2
F/A

45
BRIDGE
W.L.
All my praise and all my
Praise Team
All my praise;
Gm
Dm
B♭2
49
wor - ship comes from deep with -
Comes from deep.
F/C
C
Gm
Dm
in my soul.
B♭
Csus
C

54
INSTRUMENTAL
F
Dm
Am7

B♭2
F
3
Dm

All
D.S. al Coda
And so
B♭
C

Coda
For - ev -
B♭2

Medley options: What You Are.

Rescue me from my enemies, O LORD, for I hide myself in you. Psalm 143:9 (NIV)

I Hide Myself In Thee

11
Molto ritard
A tempo
of de-liv - er - ance; Come and sur-round me now. I hide
Bb2/D Cm/Eb Cm7 Bb2/D Eb2 Eb/F
CHORUS
1st time W.L. only
2nd time Instrumental
3rd time All
13
my - self in Thee; I hide my - self in Thee;
Bb F/A Gm7 F Eb Bb/D Cm7 F7sus Bb F/A Gm7 F
17
I hide my - self in Thee; I hide
Eb Bb/D Cm7 F7sus Bb F/A Gm7 F Eb Bb/D Cm7 F7sus
1.
my - self in Thee.
Bb F/A Gm7 F Eb Bb/D Cm7 F7sus

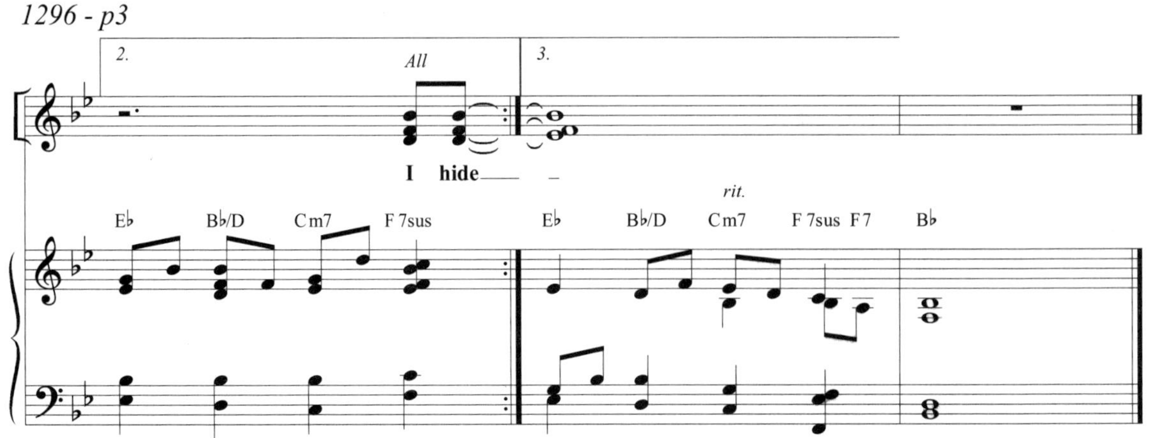

Medley options: I Look To You; Be Strong And Take Courage.

Yet I will rejoice in the LORD, I will joy in the God of my salvation. Habakkuk 3:18 (KJV)

I Will Sing

Words and Music by
DON MOEN

away, a mil - lion miles or more
to see all the thoughts and plans
F
17
it feels to - day;
You have for me;
C
G
C/G
21
Though I have - n't lost
But I will put my trust
G
Am(add2)

my faith, I must con - fess right now that it's
in You, know - ing that You died to set me free;
Am
F
C
25
hard for me to pray;
G
C/G
G
1st time W.L. only
2nd time All
29
But I don't know what to say, and I
F

33
don't know where to start; But as You give the grace,
C2/E
F
1st time All, melody only
2nd time All, add parts
Parts
with all that's in my heart; I will sing,
G
Am/G
G
37
CHORUS
I will praise,
C
F
41
e - ven in my dark - est hour, through the
Am
Em7

45
sor - row and the pain; I will sing,
F
G
C
I will praise,
lift my
F
49
last time to Coda
hands to hon - or You, be - cause Your Word is true,
Am
Em7
F
1.
53
I will sing.
G
C

Medley options: I Come to You; In the Arms of His Love.

Give unto the LORD the glory due unto his name; worship the LORD in the beauty of holiness. Psalm 29:2 (KJV)

In The Beauty Of Holiness

Words and Music by
ROBIN MARK

14
so we bring all that we pos-sess to lay at Your
that could ev-er ex-press, my King, the work that You've
A E A
feet;
done;
18
In the place where Your glo-ry shines,
Could I ev-er con-ceive of this,
E A E
2
Je-sus, lov-er of all man-kind, You have drawn us with
all the depths and the heights and breadth of the rich-es I
G#m C#m
22
love di-vine to make us com-plete.
now pos-sess be-cause of Your love.
A E A E

All
26
CHORUS
So I pause at Your gates once more as my heart and my
E
A
2
30
spir - it soar, and I wish I could love You more,
E
B
A
E
my God and my King.
1.
W.L.
Is there trib - ute that
A
E
2, 3.
35
CHORUS
So I pause at Your gates once more as my heart and my
E
E
A

2
39
spir - it soar, and I wish I could love You more,
E B A E
my God and my King.
E A E
43 INSTRUMENTAL
A E G♯m C♯m
47
A E A

Medley options: Come And Behold Him; Give Praise To Jesus.

1299

You will fill me with joy in your presence. Psalm 16:11 (NIV)

In Your Presence, O God

Words and Music by
LYNN DESHAZO

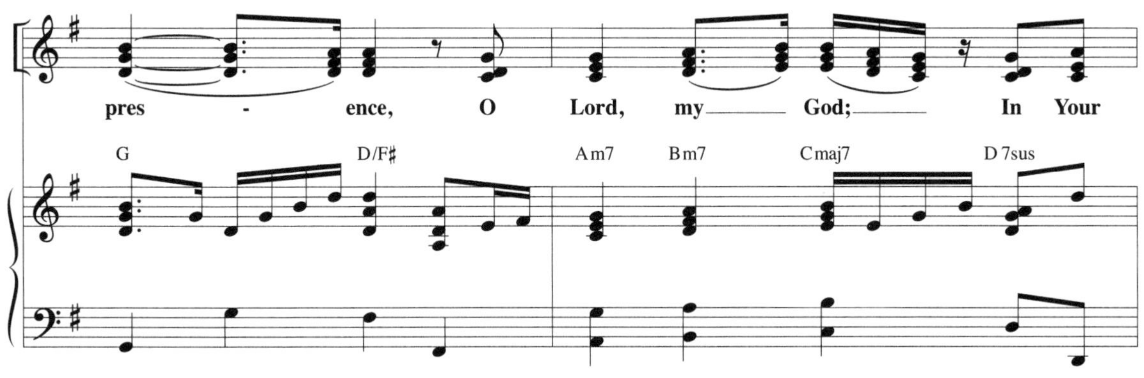

seek - ing Your face,
touch - ing Your grace,
Em7
Bm7
Em7
Bm7
10
in the cleft of the rock,
1, 2.
in Your pres - ence, O God.
C
D
Am7
G/B
C
D 7sus
In Your
C
D/C
Cmaj7
C/D
3.
16
in Your pres - ence, O God;
In Your pres - ence, O God;
C
D 7sus
Em
D
C
Dsus

Medley options: Show Me Your Face; Unto You.

....Dry bones, hear the word of the LORD....I will make breath enter you, and you will come to life. EZEKIEL 37:4,5 (NIV)

It's Time

I can hear the sound of rain;
Am7
Dsus
D
14
CHORUS
O - ver the moun - tains and o - ver the
G5
C2
18
val - leys, I hear the call - ing, it's time.
Em7
D5
G5
1. It's

24
VERSE
time, it's time for the dead to sing, it's
time, it's time for the tide to turn, it's
G
C2
27
time for the walls to ring with the songs of free-dom; It's
time for our hearts to burn with a des-per - a-tion; It's
Em7
Dsus
31
time, it's time for the numb to feel, it's
time, it's time for a sac - ri-fice, it's
G
C2
time for the wounds to heal with songs of free - dom;
time that we paid the price for our gen-er-a - tion;
Em7
Dsus

2nd time All
37
I can hear the call - ing, I can hear the
Dsus
C
Am7
sound of rain;
Dsus
D
41
CHORUS
All
O - ver the moun - tains and o - ver the
G5
C2
45
val - leys, I hear the call - ing, it's
Em7
D5

2.
time.
2. It's
G5
G5
50
CHORUS
O - ver the moun - tains and o - ver the
G5
C2
54
val - leys, I hear the call - ing, it's
Em7
D5
56
INSTRUMENTAL
Sung 1st time only
time.
G5
C

Em
D
62
1. It's
G5
66
VERSE
W.L.
time for the dead to rise, it's time for the wings to fly;
time for the numb to feel, it's time for the wounds to heal;
time that we paid the price, it's time for a sac - ri-fice;
G5
C2
70
1st time W.L. only
2nd & 3rd time All
I hear the call - ing, it's
Em7
D

Medley options: We Rejoice In You; God Is Now Reviving His People.

1301

Therefore God also has highly exalted Him and given Him the name which is above every name... Philippians 2:9 (NKJ)

Jesus, That Name

Words and Music by
TOMMY WALKER

11
1.
sound of it brings, that name high a-bove all names.
E7/G♯ F♯m7 E A F♯m7 E/B B7 E A B
2.
14 VERSE
names. No oth - er name can make the dark-ness flee; No
E F♯7 B E/B A/B F♯/B
18
oth - er name can our sal - va - tion bring; No oth - er name can set the
B E/B A/B Bm7 E7 A E/G♯
21
sin - ner free, on-ly Je - sus Christ, the
F♯m7 E/G♯ F♯/A♯ E/B B7

King.
23
INSTRUMENTAL
E
C 7sus
F
Gm7
F/A
E♭/B♭ B♭
F/C
C/B♭
F7/A
F
B♭
C
27
F
Gm7
F/A
E♭/B♭ B♭
F/C
C/B♭
F7/A Gm7
F
B♭
Gm7
31
All
No
F/C
C7
F
G

33
VERSE
oth - er name can make the dark - ness flee; No oth - er name can our sal -
C F/C B♭/C G/C C F/C
37
va - tion bring; No oth - er name can set the sin - ner
B♭/C Cm7 F7 B♭ F/A Gm7 F/A
41
free, on-ly Je - sus Christ, the King, on-ly
G/B F/C C7 Dm G B♭m/D♭
Je - sus Christ, the King, on-ly Je - sus Christ, the
F/C C C♯dim7 Dm G C♯dim7 F/C C C♯dim7

Medley options: O The Blood Of Jesus; Be Glorified.

1302

I love you, O LORD, my strength. Psalm 18:1 (NIV)

Let's Think About Our God

Who gave it all, He gave up ev - 'ry - thing; Let's think
er giv - en up, giv - en up on me or you; Let's think
says He's nev - er far from the bro - ken - heart - ed ones; Let's
Bsus B F♯m7 B7
10
a - bout the Man, Who shed His pre - cious blood, so we
a - bout our God, of love and mer - cy free, He's washed
think a - bout our Lord, Who formed the stars a - bove, so
F♯m/E E F♯m/E E
Add duet
be His friends, His friends un - til the end. And give
us white as snow for all e - ter - ni - ty.
could could have a glimpse of His glo - ry up a -
Bsus B F♯m7 B
14
CHORUS
1st time Duet
2nd time All
our love and praise to Him, He is our Sav - ior and
F♯m7 E/G♯ B 7sus B E F♯m7 E/G♯

18
our Friend; Let's give our love and praise to Him, He is
B 7sus
B
E
F♯m7
E/G♯
B 7sus
B
E
our Sav - ior and our Friend.
2. Let's think
1.
22
Female soloist
F♯m7
E/G♯
B
E
F♯m/E
2, 3.
24
All
our Friend.
We love
B
E
26
BRIDGE
You, Lord, we love You, Lord;
Just one thought of You and all
E/A
E2/G♯
F♯m7

30
we can say is, We love You, Lord, we love You, Lord;
Bsus
E/A
E2/G♯
1.
All
Just one thought of You and all we can say is, 3. Let's think
F♯m7
Bsus
2, 3.
36
we can say is, We love You, Lord, we love You, Lord;
Bsus
E/A
E2/G♯
40
Just one thought of You and all we can say is, We love You, Lord, we love
F♯m7
Bsus
E/A

last time to Coda
You, Lord;
Just one thought of You and all we can say is,
E2/G♯
F♯m7
Bsus
44
E
B/E
A/E
E
A/E
E
A/E
E
B2
1.
2.
D.S. al Coda
We love
Bsus
Coda
50
B7sus
E
B/E
A/E
E
A/E
E
A/E
E

Medley options: I Give You My Heart; Praise To You.

Lift up your heads, O you gates...that the King of glory may come in. Psalm 24:7 (NIV)

Lift Up Your Heads

Words and Music by
TOMMY WALKER

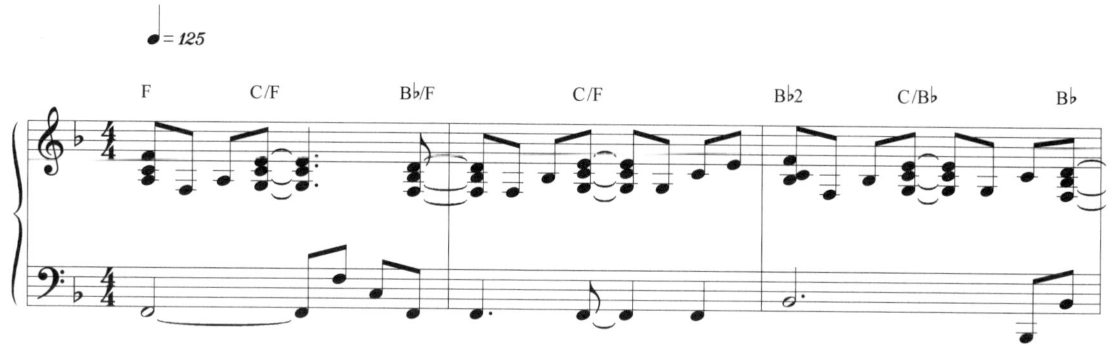

W.L.
O you gates;
Cong.
O you gates;
W.L.
Swing open wide,
C/F
Csus
C
C2
Am7
13
Cong.
Swing open wide,
W.L.
you ancient doors;
Cong.
you ancient doors;
B♭2
C/B♭
B♭
Csus
C
C2
16
W.L.
Let the King of kings
Cong.
Let the King of kings
W.L.
take His rightful place;
Csus
F
C/F
B♭/F
C/F
Cong.
take His rightful place;
W.L.
Make room, make way
21
Cong.
Make room, make way
Csus
C
C2
Am7
B♭2
C/B♭
B♭

W.L.
for our King of grace.
Cong.
24
for our King of grace.
Csus
F
C/F
B♭/F
C/F
B♭2
C/B♭
B♭
C/B♭
27
F
C/F
B♭/F
W.L.
Lift up your hands,
C/F
B♭2
C/B♭
B♭
31
CHORUS
Cong.
W.L.
o - pen up your hearts;
Lift up your hands,
F
C/F
B♭/F
C/F

Cong.
W.L.
His vict-ry o-ver sin
35
Cong.
o-pen up your hearts;
His vict-ry o-ver sin
Csus
C
C2
Am7
B♭2
C/B♭
B♭
W.L.
and death is ours;
Cong.
Duet
Let the King of kings
and death is ours;
Csus
C
C2
Csus
39
Cong.
take His right-ful place;
Cong.
Let the King of kings
take His right-ful place;
F
C/F
B♭/F
C/F
Csus
C
C2
Make room, make way
43
Cong.
for our King of grace.
Make room, make way
Am7
B♭2
C/B♭
B♭
Csus

Cong.
All
for our King of grace.
Who is this King
F C/F F Dbmaj7
47
VERSE
of glo - ry, Lord of pow'r?
Eb/Db Db Eb/Db Fm/Eb Eb Db/Eb
51
His name is Je - sus, our ris - en King;
Dbmaj7 Eb/Db Db
55
Who is this King so might -
Fsus F5 Dbmaj7 Eb/Db Db

y, Lord of strength? His name is Je -
Eb/Db
Fm/Eb
Eb
Db/Eb
Dbmaj7
59
last time to Coda
1.
sus, our ri - sen King.
Eb/Db
Db
Gm7
2.
ris - en King;
Fsus/C
F
C/F
Bb/F
C/F
Db
66
D.S. al Coda
Who is this King
Fsus
F5
Dbmaj7

Medley options: Celebrate the Lord of Love; Forever and Ever.

Those who hope in the Lord will renew their strength. They will soar on wings like eagles... Isaiah 40:31 (NIV)

Like Eagles

Words and Music by
KEVIN DUKES and MARSHA SKIDMORE

♩ = 112

3 *VERSE* *All*

F C/F B♭ B♭2 *Repeat 3 times* F

O my soul,

C Gm7 C

do you not know, have you not heard? It's been told

Coda

7

F Dm7 Gm7

from the be-gin-ning, the Lord, your God, is

11
on your side.
O my soul, don't be a-fraid,
C
F
C
hope in the Lord;
By His right-
Gm7
C
15
eous-ness and pow-er
He will strength-en, He will guide.
F
Dm7
Gm7
19
CHORUS
And I will soar on wings like ea-gles;
C
F
Dm7

23
Held by the hand of God, I will run and not
Gm7
Csus
F/A
grow tired, when on His name I call; For the Lord
Dm7
Gm7
Csus
27
is ne - ver wea - ry, His ways are be-yond
F
Dm7
Gm7
31
last time to Coda
my thoughts; I will trust in Him with all my heart.
Csus
Dm7
F2/A
Gm7
C7sus

1.
35
F
C/F
B♭
B♭2
2.
All
And
F5
39
BRIDGE
I will rest up - on His pro - mise, Pa - tient - ly I'll wait.
43

And I will soar
F
C/F
B♭
B♭2
Coda
49
I will trust in Him with
Dm
F2/A
Gm7
C 7sus
Dm7
F2/A
51
1, 2, 3.
all my heart.
Gm7
C 7sus
F
C/F
B♭
B♭2
4.
54
And I will rest up - on His pro - mise,
B♭
B♭2
B♭2

Medley options: Sing for Joy; Firm Foundation.

1305

Have mercy on us, O LORD, have mercy on us... Psalm 123:3 (NIV)

Lord Have Mercy

Words and Music by
STEVE MERKEL

9
doubt - ing heart I fol - low the paths of earth - ly wis - dom;
So now I am re - turn - ing to Your mer - cies ev - er flow - ing;
Dm B♭2 F C B♭2
For - give me for my un - be - lief, re - new the fire a - gain.
Par - don my trans - gres - sions, help me love You a - gain.
Dm B♭2 F Csus C
14 CHORUS All
Lord have mer - cy; Christ have mer - cy; Lord have mer - cy
Gm C7/E Fsus F F/A F/B♭ C Dm Gm C7sus Fsus F

18
on me; Lord have mer - cy; Christ have mer - cy;
B♭maj7 Csus C Gm C7/E Fsus F F/A F/B♭ C/E Dm
last time to Coda
21
1.
Lord have mer - cy on me.
Gm C7/E Fsus F F/B♭ C Fsus F
2.
24 INSTRUMENTAL
me.
Fsus F Dm B♭(add4) B♭ F C B♭
Dm B♭ F Csus C

30
VERSE
W.L.
I have longed to know You and all Your ten - der mer - cies, like a
Dm
B♭2
F
C
B♭2
riv - er of for - give - ness ev - er flow - ing with - out end; So I
Dm
B♭2
F
C
34
bow my heart be - fore You in the good - ness of Your pres - ence,
Dm
B♭2
F
C
B♭2
D.S. al Coda
Your grace for - ev - er shin - ing like a bea - con in the night.
Dm
B♭2
F
Csus
C

Medley options: Great Is Your Mercy; I Bow My Knee.

..."All flesh shall come to worship before me," says the LORD. Isaiah 66:23 (NKJ)

Lord, We've Come To Worship

Words and Music by
TOMMY COOMES and DON MOEN

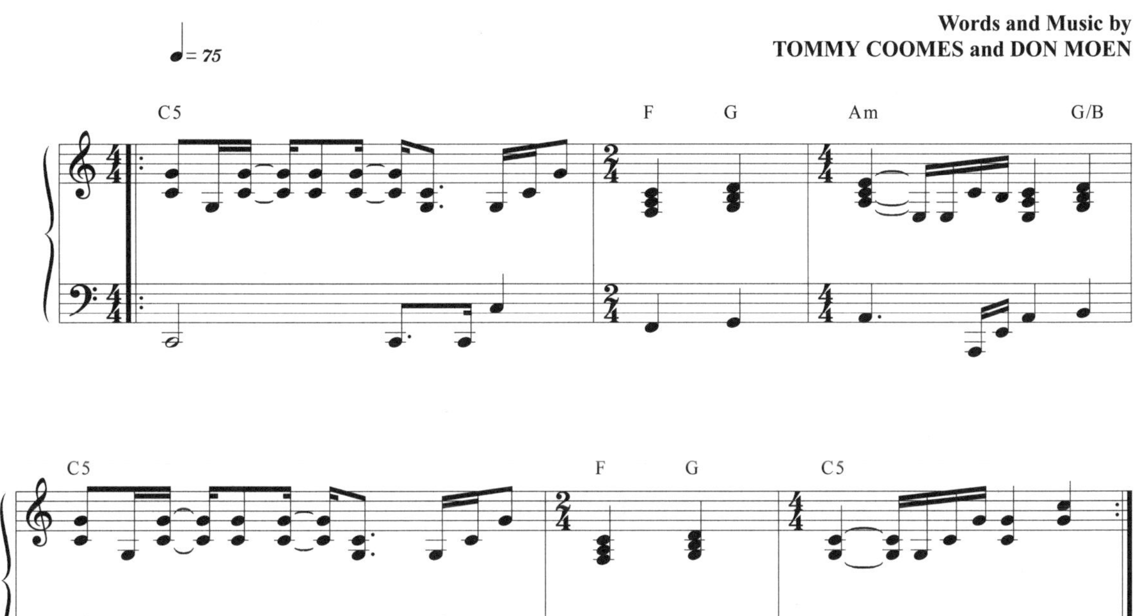

Lord, we've come to list - en, and
Look down in ten - der mer - cy, for -
Am
G/B
C5
hear what You would say;
give our sins, we pray;
O
F
G
C
13
Lord, our hearts are long - ing to meet with You to - day;
Lord, we need re - viv - al, all a - cross this land;
C5
F
G
1.
For we have come to seek You, and
Come
Am
G/B
C5

we have come to say
F
G
C
B♭
19
CHORUS
Worth - y, You are worth - y, King of
F
B♭
kings, Lord of lords; You are worth - y; All
C
Fsus
F
C/E
23
bless-ing and pow - er, all rich-es and wis - dom, all glo-ry and hon - or and praise
Dm
B♭
Gm7

27
to the Lamb.
Csus
C
F
G
2.
move a-mong Your peo-ple, with Your might-y hand.
C5
F
G
32 CHORUS
Worth-y, You are
C
D
G
worth-y, King of kings, Lord of lords; You are
C
D

worth - y; All
Gsus
G
D/F♯
36
bless - ing and pow - er, all rich - es and wis - dom, all
Em
C
glo - ry and hon - or and praise To the Lamb
Am7
Dsus
40
BRIDGE
that was slain to re -
G
Gsus
G
C2

deem us back to God a - gain; To the Lamb
D
G5
44
Who will reign for - ev - er and ev - er, a -
G Gsus G
C2
D
1, 2.
3.
men. To the Lamb men; For -
G
Em D C G/B
ev - er and ev - er, a - men;
51
For - ev - er and ev - er, for -
Am7 D Em D C G/B Am7 G/B

Medley options: Our Heart; Jesus, We Enthrone You.

1307

For the LORD is good; His mercy is everlasting... Psalm 100:5 (NKJ)

Lord, You Are Good

not been by my side?
How could I rise to meet the
Bb/D
Bbm/Db
F/C
G/B
13
morn-ing of the day,
Your ten-der mer-cy al-ways call-
Gm7
C 7sus
F
F/Eb
2nd time Duet
ing from be-hind;
At times I could not see You, e-ven
Bb/D
Bbm/Db
F/C
G/B
3rd time Vocals reenter
though You were close by.
And
Gm7
C
F

18
CHORUS
All
Lord, You are good, You are good, and Your mer-
F/E♭
B♭/D
B♭m/D♭
F/C
cy for - ev - er en - dures; O
Gm7
C 7sus
F
22
Lord, You are good, You are good, and Your mer-
F/E♭
B♭/D
B♭m/D♭
F/C
last time to Coda
2.
cy for - ev - er en - dures.
Gm7
C 7sus
F B♭/F F
F B♭/F F
3

27
BRIDGE
All
Help me to see Your lov - ing - kind - ness;
Gm7
F/A
B♭
F/A
Help me to see You as You are;
31
P.T. Men add harmonies
Help me to see Your lov-ing-kind -
Gm7
F/A
Csus
C
Gm7
F/A
ness;
Help me to see You as You
B♭
F/A
Gm7
F/A
All
D.S. al Coda
are,
as You real - ly, real - ly are.
Csus
C
Csus
C

CHORUS
37
Coda
O Lord, You are good,
F Bb/F F F/Eb Bb/D
You are good, and Your mer - cy for - ev - er en - dures;
Bbm/Db F/C Gm7 C 7sus
41
O Lord, You are good,
F F/Eb Bb/D
You are good, and Your mer - cy for - ev - er en - dures.
Bbm/Db F/C Gm7 C 7sus

Medley options: You Are Good; He's Been Good.

1308

For God so loved the world that he gave his one and only Son.... JOHN 3:16 (NIV)

Love Came Down

Words and Music by
LINDELL COOLEY and LENNY LeBLANC

13
but we all went wrong;
no more chains on me,
Then a Sav - ior came and He took
since the Sav - ior came and He took
F♯m7
G
D
Add Praise Team Men, upper note
the blame, changed ev - 'ry - thing;
the blame, changed ev - 'ry - thing;
Then a Sav -
Since the Sav -
A
G
17
All, melody bottom note
ior came and He took the blame, changed ev - 'ry - thing.
ior came and He took the blame, changed ev - 'ry - thing.
D
A
G
21
CHORUS
I could sing a - bout His for - give - ness,
D
A

25
I could praise Him 'til the sun goes down; I can say that
Em7
G
D
I am a wit - ness, I was there when His love came down,
A
Em7
G
29
1.
Melody middle note
love came down on me,
D
A
Em7
33
love came down on me.
D
A

37
Em7
Am/D
D
1.
Asus
A
G
Gsus
G
Gsus
G
41
2, 3. CHORUS
I could sing a - bout His for - give - ness, I could praise Him 'til the
D
A
Em7
45
sun goes down;
I can say that I am a wit - ness,
G
D
A

49
Melody middle note
I was there when His love came down,
love came
Em7
G
D
down on me,
A
Em7
Em7
53
love came down on me.
D
A
Em7
Repeat Verse 2
57
BRIDGE
W.L.
Love came down like a rush - ing riv - er;
Em7
D
A

P.T.
Love came down on me;
Em7
61
W.L.
2nd time W.L. ad libs
Love came down and it broke through my dark - ness;
His
D
A/D
Em7
1.
love came down on me.
2.
love came down on me.
Em7
Sing 1st time only
1, 2, 3.
D
A
Em7

Medley options: Your Love For Me; Only A God Like You.

Who is this King of glory? The LORD strong and mighty, the LORD mighty in battle. Psalm 24:8 (NIV)

Mighty King

Words and Music by
TONY SUTHERLAND

mountains shake; The whole earth will fall at Your feet. You are the
enemies, and You'll reign for - ev - er - more.
E♭ B♭ G♭maj7 Caug7(♯9)
13 CHORUS
All W.L. All
mighty - y King; Let all the peo - ple sing to the King of Glo -
D♭maj7 E♭ Fm D♭maj7 E♭ Fm D♭maj7
W.L. 17 All W.L.
ry; You are the might - y King, awe - some in ev - 'ry - thing,
E♭ D♭maj7 E♭ Fm
All last time to Coda W.L. 2.
Might - y King of Glo - ry. All of cre– - ry.
D♭maj7 E♭ Fm E♭ E♭

22
BRIDGE
P.T. Ladies
W.L. ad libs
We praise the might - y King; We praise the
B♭m9
25
1, 2, 3.
might - y King.
4.
W.L. You are the
D.S. al Coda
might - y King.
B♭m9
B♭m9
⊕ Coda
28
CHORUS
W.L.
ry. Might - y King; Let all the peo - ple sing
E♭
D♭maj7 E♭ Fm
All
W.L.
32
All
to the King of Glo - ry; You are the might - y King,
D♭maj7 E♭ Fm D♭maj7
E♭
D♭maj7 E♭ Fm

Medley options: Mighty God.

In the last days, God says, I wil pour out my Spirit on all people... Acts 2:17 (NIV)

Move, Spirit, Move

Words and Music by
TONY SUTHERLAND

3
moun - tains might shake as Your glo - ry comes down; We've
we don't have You, then where can we go; We're
F/G
C/G
D/G
14
heard of Your won - ders, Your works and Your ways; We're
an - ti - ci - pat - ing all that You'll do;
G
D/G
2nd time All
des - p'rate for You, Lord, to move in our day.
Turn to our cry, Lord, we're turn - ing to You.
F/G
Am7 G/B C Am7/D
19
CHORUS
All
W.L.
Move, Spir - it, move; We want You to
G
D/F♯
Em
D/F♯
E/G♯

All
23
W.L.
move, Spir - it, move; Move in us, a-mong us, and
Am G/B C D G
3
touch the world through us; With - out You we can't find our way;
Bm7 Em Am7 G/B G/C D D/E Em7
27
All
Move, Spir - it, move to - day.
Am7 G/B G/C D Am/D G D/F#
3
30
1.
Em7 Am7 C/D

2.
34
BRIDGE
Praise Team
W.L. ad libs
Oo,
oo;
C/D
G/C
Bm7
38
Oo,
Oo;
Oo,
G/C
Bm7
Baug7
G/C
Oo;
Oo,
Oo;
Bm7
G/C
B7
Baug7
42
Move, Ho - ly Spir - it, we're wait - ing on You; Move, Ho - ly Spir - it, we're
Em
Bm7
Em

46
wait-ing on You; Move, Ho - ly Spir - it, we're wait-ing on You; Fill our
Bm7
Em
Bm7
hearts, fill our minds, Spir - it move.
Cmaj7
Baug7
D/E
50
CHORUS
All
W.L.
All
Move, Spir - it, move; Won't You move, Spir - it,
A
E/G♯
F♯m
E/G♯
F♯/A♯
Bm
A/C♯
D
54
W.L.
3
move; Move in us, a-mong us, and touch the world through us; With-
E
A
C♯m7
F♯m

Medley options: My Heart Will Trust.

I will praise you as long as I live... Psalm 63:4 (NIV)

My Quiet Place

Words and Music by
SAM KENOLY

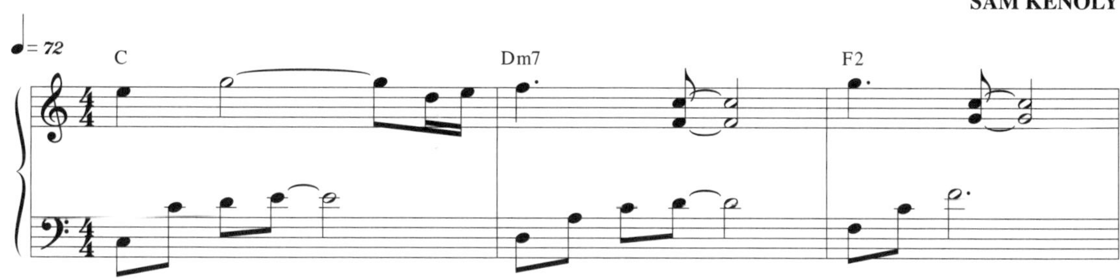

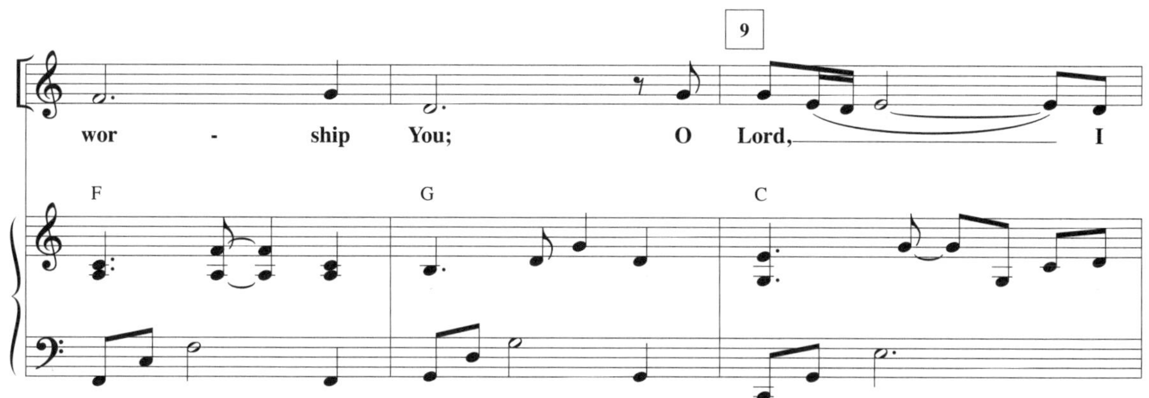

love to wor - ship You; You have
Dm7
F
G
13
giv - en me so much to be thank - ful
Am
Em7
F
for, and I love You is not e - nough to ex -
17
C
G/B
Am
Em7
press my love; Ev - 'ry - thing I have in -
21
F
C
G/B
Am

side of me, Lord, I give to You; There is
Em7
F
C
25
noth - ing I can do; There is noth - ing I can do;
Dm7
G
G/F
Em7
29
There is noth - ing I can do but wor - ship
A 7sus
A
Dm7
G
33 CHORUS
You. O Lord, I
C
A 7sus
D

love to wor - ship You; O
Em7(add4)
G
A
37
Lord, I love to wor - ship
D
Em7
G
41
You; You have giv - en me so much to be
A
Bm
F♯m7
45
thank - ful for, and my words are not e -
G
D
A/C♯
Bm

nough to ex - press my love; Ev - 'ry -
F♯m7
G
D
A/C♯
49
thing I have in - side of me, Lord, I give to You;
Bm
F♯m7
G
53
There is noth - ing more to do; There is
D
Em7
Asus
A
57
noth - ing more to do; There is noth - ing more to
F♯m7
B7sus
B
Em7

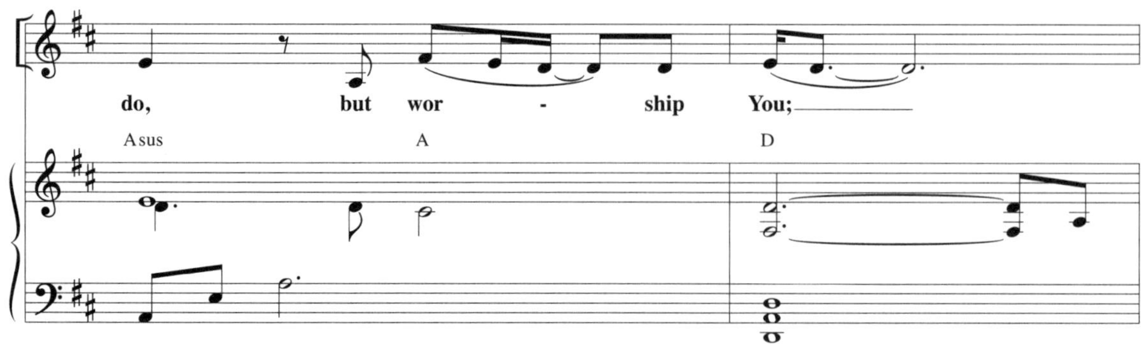

Medley options: I Love To Be With You; A Place At Your Altar.

I will praise you forever for what you have done... Psalm 52:9 (NIV)

Never Gonna Stop

Words and Music by
TOMMY WALKER

13

For the story of Your love, for the

B7(♯9) Em7 Am7 D9

17

wonder of Your blood, how it makes the sinner clean,

Am7 Em7 Am7 G/B

All

someone like me. So, I'm

C G Em7 C

21 𝄋 **CHORUS**
3rd time vocals only

never gonna stop, never gonna stop, lifting up my hands to You, lifting

G D Am7 G/B C G D

25
up my heart; When the last day comes and goes, and time will be no more,
Am7
G/B
C
G
D
Am7
G/B
3rd time band reenters
29
I'll be prais - ing You; No, I'll nev - er let it end, I'll just be -
C
A/C♯
Dsus
D
G
D
gin it all a - gain; Shouts of thank - ful - ness and love I'm al - ways gon - na give; A
Am7
G/B
C
G
D
Am7
G/B
C
33
thou - sand years from now, be - fore Your throne of grace and pow'r, I'll be prais - ing You,
G
D
Am7
G/B
C
A/C♯

last time to Coda
1.
praising You.
Dsus
D
G
D
2.
39
G
D
Am7
G/B C
G
D
Am7
42
BRIDGE
Though pressed on ev'ry side, with
D
C2
troubles and fears so near me; And should the whole wide world deny
D
C2
46
D

Medley options: The Solid Rock (HARRIS); Glorious God.

1313

....For there is none like You, nor is there any God besides You.... 2 Samuel 7:22 (NKJ)

No One Like You, Lord

Words and Music by
ROBIN MARK

9
a sure found - a - tion when the sand is sink - ing,
but ev - 'ry chain of sin and death You've bro - ken,
For - ev - er plead - ing for the souls You've cap - tured,
Oo;
G
D/G
C/G
All
where we are built up - on like liv - ing stones. There is
and tri - umphed o - ver by Your might - y pow'r.
for - ev - er watch - ing as You call us home.
G
13
CHORUS
no one else like You, there is no one like You, Lord;
C
G
C

17
There is no one else like You, Son of Man
G
C
Em
C
21
last time to Coda
and Son of God, Son of Man and Son of God.
G
D
G
C
G
D
1.
2.
W.L.
I want to run
G
D/G
C/G
G
25
BRIDGE
the race You've set be - fore me,
Bm7
C
G
C/G

29
e - ven to share
in the
suf - f'ring
of
the
cross,
G
Bm7
C
33
that I might
gain
the prize
D
Bm7
for which
You
called
me,
to
be with
C
G
C/G
G
37
You,
Son of
Man
and Son of
God,
C
D
Em

Add male soloist, lower note
41
to be with You, Son of Man and Son of God.
Em
C
D
G
D/G
C/G
D.S. al Coda
Coda
W.L.
46
CHORUS
All
There is no one else like You, there is
no one like You, Lord; There is
50
no one else like You,

Medley options: Shine, Jesus, Shine; He Shall Reign (CHOPINSKY).

1314

....'Not by might nor by power, but by my Spirit,' says the LORD Almighty. Zechariah 4:6 (NIV)

Not By Might

Words and Music by
ROBIN MARK

Spir - it, O Lord;
G
C
13
Heal - er of hearts, bind - er of
C
G
17
wounds, lives that are lost re -
C
D
21
stored; Flow through this
G
C

land
'til ev - 'ry man
G
25
prais - es Your name once more.
C
D
G
Repeat as desired
29
Flow through this
C
land
'til ev - 'ry man
G

Medley options: Holy Spirit, Rain Down; Let Your Glory Fall.

1315

My flesh and my heart may fail, but God is the strength of my heart and my portion forever. Psalm 73:26 (NIV)

Oil Of Your Spirit

Words and Music by
KRISTI NORTHUP and LINDELL COOLEY

10
the wind that blows a - cross my soul will
Your will I've cho - sen as my own, but I am
D A Bm
make me whole;
so a - lone;
So while I wait for You,
I know I've strayed be - fore,
D/G G G2 G C
14
Your love will bring me through
but now I'm want - ing more
G/B C
18
and I will be changed.
than more of the same.
G/B G Bm A Asus A

20
CHORUS
All
Give me the oil of Your Spir - it, pour o - ver me, cov - er me;
G D/F♯ Em D A F♯/A♯
24
You are my strength and my por - tion; I am so weak,
Bm A G D/F♯ Em D
last time to Coda
28
but all that I need I find sim - ply in who You are.
A C2 G/B A 7sus
1.
2.
D.S. al Coda
D A Bm G D

Medley options: Redeemer, Savior, Friend; My Heart, Your Home.

Praise the LORD, for the LORD is good... Psalm 135:3 (NIV)

Only A God Like You

Words and Music by
TOMMY WALKER

♩ = 108

G D Em

1. 2. All

6 VERSE

For the prais - es of man,

C C G

10
king - doms of this world, I'll nev - er give my heart a - way or shout
G
D
C2
14
my praise; My al - le - giance and de - vo - tion, my heart's de -
Dsus
D
G
D
18
sire and all e - mo - tion, go to serve the Man Who died
Em
C
G
up - on that tree.
D
C2
Dsus
D

22
CHORUS
On-ly a God like You could be worth - y of my praise, and all my hope and faith; To on-ly a King of all kings, do I bow my knee and sing, give my ev-'ry-thing; On-ly a God like You could be worth - y of my praise, and all my hope and faith; To
G
D
Bm7
Em7
C
26
30

34
on-ly a King of all kings, do I bow my knee and sing, give
G D Bm7 Em7
38
my ev-'ry-thing; To on-ly my Mak - er, my Fa - ther, my Sav - ior, Re-
C Am7 G/B C Em7
deem - er, Re - stor - er, Re - build - er, Re - ward - er; To
Am7 G/B C Em7
42
on-ly a God like You, do I give my praise.
Am7 C Dsus D G

46
1.
For the
D
Em
C
2.
49
C
G
D
Em
53
VERSE
Worship Leader
On - ly the God, Who left His throne a - bove, He came to
C
G
D
57
live with us,___ came to be one of us;___ To on - ly the One,___Who stopped to
Em
C
G

heal that blind man, took the time to save that one lost lamb;
D
Em
C
61
To on - ly the King, Who wore that crown of thorns so I
G
D
B7(b9)
could wear the crown of life; And to on-ly the One, Who con-quered
Em
C
65
G
sin and death so we could be set free, so we could stand here and sing.
D
Em
C2

69
BRIDGE
All
W.L. ad libs
On - ly a God like You, on - ly a God like You,
G
D
1, 2, 3.
on - ly a God like You.
Em7
C
4.
75
on - ly a God like You. To on - ly my Mak - er, my Fa -
Em7
C
Am7
G/B
ther, my Sav - ior, Re - deem - er, Re - stor - er, Re - build - er, Re - ward - er; To
C
Em7
Am7
G/B
C
Em7

Medley options: Whom Shall I Fear; On Our Side.

1317

...."Look! I see the heavens opened and the Son of Man standing at the right hand of God!" Acts 7:56 (NKJ)

Open Up The Sky

Words and Music by
LINDELL COOLEY and LENNY LeBLANC

13
My life is filled with ev - 'ry - thing but You;
soon we're gon - na see Your king - dom come;
Gsus G C
17
Lord, I real - ly want
Can you hear the sound
G Am7
to see Your glo - ry;
of des - per - a - tion, a
D Dsus D
21
Let the fire of Heav - en fall on me.
prayer on the lips of ev - 'ry na - tion.
Am7 C D

All
25 CHORUS
1. Can You feel my pas - sion, can You see my
2, 3. Can You feel our pas - sion, can You see our
G2
29
hun - ger, do You know how I long
hun - ger, do You know how we long
Em7
C
for You; No walls be -
for You; No walls be -
D
C/E
33
tween us, take a - way this dark - ness,
tween us, take a - way this dark - ness,
G2
Em7

37
come break this heart of stone;
come break these hearts of stone;
C
D
last time to Coda
Hear my cry, o - pen up the sky.
Hear our cry, o - pen up the sky.
Am7
G/B
C
42
G2
Em7
46
C2
G5
1.
2.

51
BRIDGE
W.L.
Lord, we real - ly want to see Your glo - ry;
Am7
D
55
Let the fire of Heav - en fall on me.
Dsus
D
Am7
C
Ê
D
All
D.S. al Coda
Can You feel our
Coda
60
CHORUS
Can You feel our pas - sion,
can You see our
C
G2

64
hun - ger,
do You know how we long
Em7
C
for
You;
No walls be -
D
C/E
68
tween us,
take a - way this dark - ness,
G2
Em7
72
come break these hearts of stone;
C
D

Medley options: Rise Up And Praise Him; All The Power You Need.

"Our Father in heaven, hallowed be your name." Matthew 6:9 (KJV)

Our Father

Words and Music by
DON MOEN

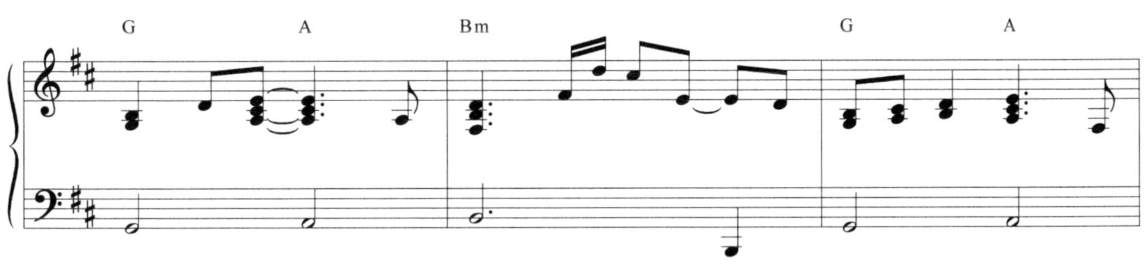

9
we are Your child - ren, and we've gath-ered here to-day; We've
es to Heav-en; May Your glo-ry fill the earth as the
G D G A Bm
gath - er'd here to pray;
13
Hear our cry,
All
wat - ers cov - er the sea;
See our hearts
G A D
14
we need Your mer - cy, and we need Your grace to-day,
and re-move an - y - thing that is stand - ing in the way
D G D G A

17
All
hear us as we pray. Our
of com - ing to You to - day. Our
Bm
G
A
D

CHORUS
21
Fa - ther, Who art in Heav-en, Hal-low-ed be Thy name;
A
Bm
G
D
A

25
Our Fa - ther, hear us from Heav-en;
D
A
Bm
G

1.
W.L. & P.T. Ladies
For-give our sins, we pray.
2) Hear our song
D
A
D
2.
29
30
BRIDGE
Though we are few
we're sur-round - ed by ma-ny
who have
D
A
Bm
G
33
34
crossed that riv - er be-fore,
and this is the song
we'll be sing -
D
A
D
A
37
ing for-ev-er,
Ho - ly is the Lord;
Bm
G
D
A
Bm

Ho - ly is the Lord.
Ho - ly is the Lord;
G
A
Bm
G
A
41
Praise Team Men
Ho - ly is the Lord;
Ho - ly is the Lord;
Ho - ly is the
Bm
G
A
Bm
A
45
Ho - ly is the Lord;
Ho - ly is the Lord.
Lord;
Ho - ly is the Lord.
G
A
Bm
A
G
A

W.L.

49 VERSE

1.) Hear our prayer,

D Bb Eb

we are Your child - ren, and we've gath - ered here to - day; We've

Ab Eb Ab Bb Cm

W.L. & P.T. Ladies 55 W.L.

gath - er'd here to pray; Hear our cry, O Lord,

Ab Bb Eb Eb

W.L. & P.T. Ladies 57

we need Your mer - cy, and we need Your grace to - day,

Ab Eb Ab Bb Cm

All
61
CHORUS
hear us as we pray.
Our Fa - ther,
A Few Voices
Our Fa-ther;
Ab
Bb
Eb
Bb
Cm
Who art in Heav-en,
Hal-low-ed be Thy name;
Our
O, our
Ab
Eb
Bb
Eb
65
1.
Fa - ther,
hear us from Heav-en;
For-give our sins, we pray.
our Fa - ther,
Bb
Cm
Ab
Eb
Bb

Medley options: You Are Here; I Will Never Be

...Stand up and praise the LORD your God, who is from everlasting to everlasting. Nehemiah 9:5 (NIV)

Praise Him

Words and Music by
SAM KENOLY

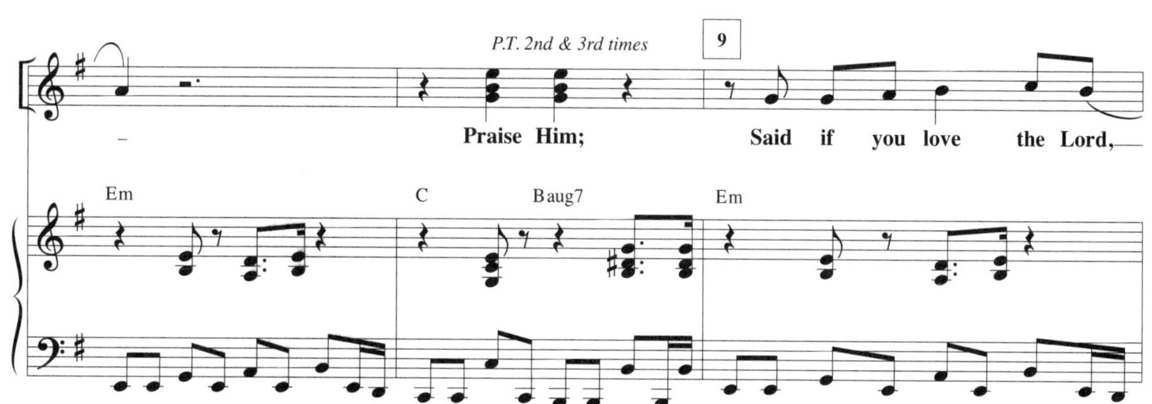

1.
W.L.
stand on your feet, come on;
The Lord is wor -
C
Baug7
Em
13
Male P.T. Soloist
thy; The Lord is wor - thy of our praise;
Am7
D/E
17
The Lord is wor - thy of our praise.
N.C.
F♯
A7
2.

22
Em
C
Baug7
Em
C
Baug
3.
C
Baug7
W.L.
27
Male P.T. Soloist
Am7
The Lord is wor - thy; The Lord is wor -
thy of our praise;
D/E
Em
Am7
N.C.
31
The Lord is wor - thy of our praise.
Am7
D/E
Em
F♯

35
CHORUS
W.L.
P.T.
So stand up! Stand up and give Him praise, come on and give Him the praise;
A7
Em
C
Baug7
39
Praise Him!
Stand up and give Him praise,
come on and give Him the praise.
43
INSTRUMENTAL
W.L. ad libs

47
BRIDGE
W.L.
P.T.
God has been good to me, God has been good to me,
Em
W.L.
P.T.
W.L.
God has been good to me, God has been good to me; Ha - le - lu -
Em
51
P.T.
W.L.
jah, hal - le - lu - jah, hal - le - lu - jah; Hal - le - lu -
Em
PT
jah, hal - le - lu - jah, hal - le - lu - jah.
Em

Medley options: Stand Up And Give Him The Praise; Not By Power.

"...Prepare the way of the Lord; Make straight in the desert a highway for our God." Isaiah 40:3 (NKJ)

Prepare The Way

Words and Music by
DARRELL EVANS and ERIC NUZUM

10
to bring free - dom to the cap -
to com - fort all who mourn;
G
F
14
tives; He has come to re -
He has come to
C
G/B
Am
G
F
2nd Time All
18
store the bro - ken-heart - ed; It's time to pro - claim
heal our ev - 'ry sick - ness; It's time to pro - claim
C
Gsus
Dm7
1st time W.L.
2nd Time All
the year of the Lord.
the year of the Lord.
Pre-pare the way,
F
C
Gsus

22
CHORUS
Praise Team
pre - pare the way for our Re - deem -
Pre - pare the way;
C
F
Am
26
er; Pre - pare the way,
pre - pare the way
Pre - pare the way;
F
C
F
All
30
for our Re - stor - er;
Make read - y your heart, make
Am
F
Dm7

1.
read - y your home, make read - y the peo - ple of God; Pre - pare the way.
C/E
F
Gsus
34
C2
W.L.
2. He has come
2.
W.L.
D.S.
God; Pre - pare the way,
Gsus
3.
40
God; Pre - pare the way.
Gsus
C2

44
BRIDGE
C5
F2/D
C/E
F2
48
C/G
Am7
Dm7
W.L.
52
Pre - pare,
pre - pare,
pre - par -
F
C
F2/D
56
ing the way of the Lord;
Pre - pare,
pre - pare,
P.T.
Pre - pare,
C/E
F2
C/G

pre - pare.
Pre - pare the way,
pre - pare,
pre - pare.
Am7
C/E
Gsus
60
CHORUS
pre - pare the way for our Re - deem -
Pre - pare the way;
D
G
Bm
64
er; Pre - pare the way,
pre - pare the way
Pre - pare the way;
G
D
G

Medley options: Thine Is The Kingdom; He Will Come And Save You; Over And Over.

1321

He brought streams also out of the rock, and caused waters to run down like rivers. Psalm 78:16 (KJV)

River Of Love

Words and Music by
CLAIRE CLONINGER and DON MOEN

14
more of Your Spir - it and
save me and I will be
C
G
18
truth; Wash me from
saved; You've filled me with
A
D
22
all my sin, and fill me
songs of praise; For - ev - er
A
C
with Your Spir - it a - gain. You're the
I will sing of Your grace. You're the
G
A

26
CHORUS
Riv - er of love,
flow - ing with grace
and mer - cy,
2nd & 3rd times A Few Voices
Ri - ver of love;
Bm
F♯m7
30
flood - ing my soul,
fill - ing my heart
O;
Gmaj7
34
with peace;
O,
Riv - er of love,
F♯sus
F♯
Bm

like streams in the des - ert,
Ri - ver of love;
F♯m7
38
All
last time to Coda
Giv - er of life,
Giv - ing Your life
and
Gmaj7
F♯sus
42
1.
love to set me free.
F♯
Bm
A/C♯
2.
45
BRIDGE
If an - y - one is thirst - y let him
Bm
A
G

49
come on in;
When you drink the liv - ing wat -
Bm
A
er,
you will nev - er thirst a - gain.
O.
G
F♯
53 Instrumental
Bm
Gmaj7
57
Bm
Gmaj7

61
Em7
F♯sus
F♯
65
Gmaj7
Asus
A
69
Bm
Gmaj7
Em7
F♯sus
F♯7
73
Gmaj7
Asus
A
Em7
Bm
Asus
A
D.S. al Coda
Coda
78
CHORUS
love; O, River of love,
flowing with grace
Ri - ver of love;
F♯
Bm

82
and mer-cy,
flood-ing my soul,
fill-ing my heart
O;
F♯m7
Gmaj7
86
with
peace;
O,
Riv-er
of love,
F♯sus
F♯
Bm
like
streams
in the des-ert,
Ri-ver
of love;
F♯m7

90
All
Giv - er of life,
Giv - ing Your life
and
Gmaj7
F♯sus
94
love to set me free.
Giv - ing Your life
F♯
Bm
98
and love to set me free.
F♯sus
F♯
Bm
Giv - ing Your life
and love to set me free.
F♯sus
F♯

Medley options: Join Our Hearts; Faithful And Just.

I seek you with all my heart; do not let me stray from your commands. Psalm 119:10 (NIV)

Seek Your Face

Words and Music by
CLINT BROWN & DAVID BINION

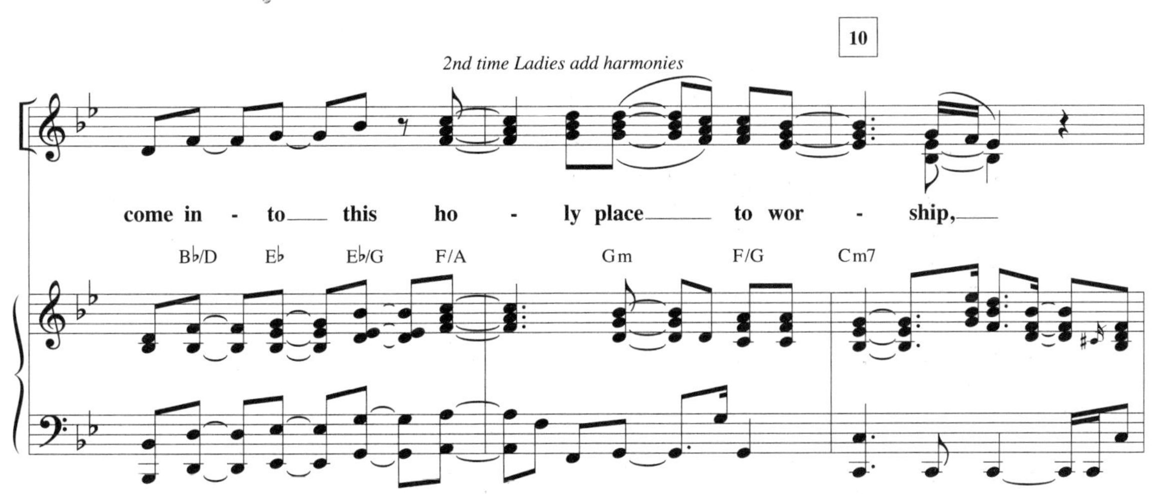

to wor-ship You.
Eb/F
Bb
Eb
Bb
Eb2
14
W.L.
Lord, I long to seek Your face;
I've come in - to this ho -
Bb
Eb
F
Bb
Bb
Eb
18
ly place to wor - ship,
to wor-ship You.
F
Gm
Cm7
Eb/F
All
21
VERSE
W.L.
A place where Your glo - ry sur-rounds me and
Bb
Cm7
Bb/D
Ebmaj7
F/Eb
Dm7
Gm

All
25
I be - come brand new; A place where Your pres - ence brings rev' -
Cm7 E♭/F B♭ Cm7 B♭/D E♭maj7 F/E♭

1.
rence; I de - sire to be with You.
Dm7 Gm Cm7 B♭/D E♭ F7sus

2.
W.L.
30
BRIDGE
with You. For when I'm with You, I am com-plete; My world
P.T. Ladies
Oo,
E♭ F Gm D/F♯

34
stops turn-ing when You're hold-ing me; Lord, my de-sire (re) is to
Oo;
B♭/F
C/E
Cm7
be in Your pre - sence, so I'm run-ning to You for an-oth-er touch of Hea-ven.
Touch;
B♭/D
E♭maj7
F 7sus
39 INSTRUMENTAL
P.T. Ladies
Hea-ven;
N.C.
C
F
G
C

C F G Am
43
Dm7
45
CHORUS
P.T.
W.L. ad libs
Lord, I long to seek Your face; I've
F/G C F G C
49
come in - to this ho - ly place to wor - ship,
C F G Am Dm7
1.
2.
52
wor - ship.
to wor - ship,
F/G F/G Dm7

Medley options: I'm Talking 'Bout Jesus.

Now therefore, I pray, if I have found grace in Your sight, show me now Your way, that I may know You and that I may find grace in Your sight... Exodus 33:13 (NKJ)

Show Me Your Face

Words and Music by
DON POTTER

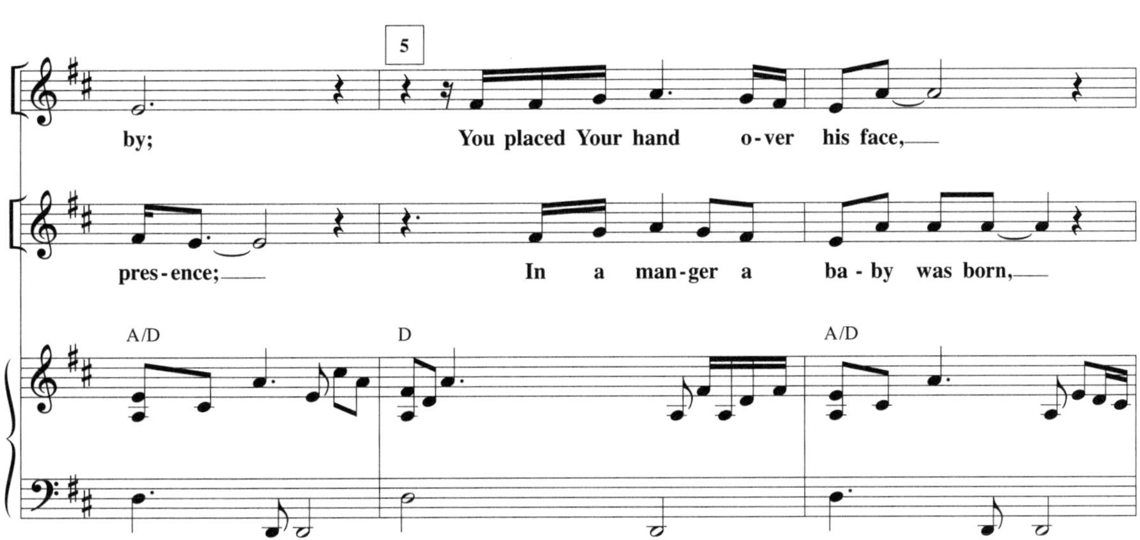

9
in Your pres - ence he would - n't die; All Is - ra - el
3
a - mongst kings and peas - ants; All Is - ra - el
G/D
A/D
A/G
saw Your glo - ry, and it shines down through the age;
F♯m7
Bm
F♯m/A
G
D/F♯
13
Now You've called us to bold - ly seek Your face.
Em7
G/A

All
Show me Your face,
D
17 CHORUS
W.L.
Lord;
Show me Your face
Gmaj7
A/G
F♯m7
1st time Worship Leader
2nd & 3rd times add Male soloist
21
and then gird up my legs that I might stand in this ho - ly
Bm
Em7
G/A
All
25
place;
Show me Your face,
Lord,
D
Gmaj7

W.L.
Your pow - er and Your grace; I will
G F♯ F♯/A♯ Bm D/A A G D/F♯
29
1.
31
make it to the end if I could just see Your face.
Em7 A 7sus G A/G
Gmaj7 A/G G A/G Gmaj7 A 7sus
2.
36
All
D.S.
if I could just see Your face. Show me Your face,
A 7sus D

Medley options: Highest Place; Here In Your Presence.

1324

Sing for joy to God our strength; shout aloud to the God of Jacob! Psalm 81:1 (NIV)

Sing For Joy

Words and Music by
LAMONT HIEBERT

13
If we lift our hands, He will lift us up;
He will heal our hearts, He will cleanse our hands;
E
A
17
Come now, praise His name, all you saints of God.
If we rend our hearts, He will heal our land.
E
B
E A/E
19 CHORUS
O sing for joy to
E A/E
E
A
23
God, our strength; O sing for
E
B
E

joy to God, our strength, our
A E B
27
strength.
E A/E E A/E
29 VERSE
1) If we call to Him, He will ans - wer us; If we run to Him,
2) Draw near to Him, He is here with us; Give Him your love,
G C G
He will run to us; If we lift our hands, He will lift us up;
He's in love with us; He will heal our hearts, He will cleanse our hands;
D G C
33

37
Come now, praise His name, all you saints of God.
If we rend our hearts, He will heal our land.
G
D
G
C/G
1.
2.
O
G
C/G
G
C/G
40
CHORUS
3rd time rhythm only
sing for joy to God, our
G
C
G
44
strength; O sing for joy to
D
G
C

Medley options: Firm Foundation; The River Is Here.

Bless the LORD, O my soul; and all that is within me, bless his holy name. Psalm 103:1 (KJV)

Sing Of Your Great Love

Words and Music by
DARLENE ZSCHECH

11
brought me out of dark - ness and in - to Your glor - i - ous light; For -
E2
B(add4)
ev - er I will sing of Your great love; For -
A
B(add4)
C♯m
E/B
15
ev - er I will sing of Your great love.
A2
B(add4)
E5
VERSE
1st time All, melody only
2nd time add harmonies
18
I love to see You glor - i - fied, to
E

see You lift - ed high; I yearn to see all na - tions bow their
B(add4)
C♯m
B(add4)
22
knee; It's You a - lone, Lord Je - sus, Who can
A2
E2
cause the cold - est heart to find Your love and ev - er - last - ing
B(add4)
A
B(add4)
26
1st time add parts
peace, to find Your love and ev - er - last - ing
C♯m
E/B
A2
B(add4)

peace.
E5
29
CHORUS
All
Ho - ly,
ho - ly,
ho - ly is the
E/A
E/G♯
F♯m7
33
Lord;
Ho - ly,
ho - ly,
C♯m
E/G♯
E/A
E/G♯
37
ho - ly is the Lord;
Ho - ly,
F♯m7(add4)
B(add4)
A
E
E/A

holy, holy is the Lord;
E/G♯
F♯m7
C♯m
E/G♯
41
last time to Coda
Holy, holy, holy is the
E/A
E/G♯
F♯m7(add4)
B(add4)
1.
45
Lord.
A2
E(add2)
All
2.
W.L.
I Lord. For Your
A2
8va

50
BRIDGE
Molto rubato
3
trum - pet will sound, and all the heav - ens will know that the
A2
E/G♯
54
time has fin - 'ly come for Your bride to
F♯m7
C♯m
A2
A tempo
D.S. al Coda
take her place; and we'll hear the an - gels sing.
E/G♯
F♯m7(add4)
C♯m
Coda
Lord.
A2
8va

Medley options: Be Glorified; O God You Are My God (WRIGHT).

The Spirit of the Sovereign LORD is on me, because the LORD has anointed me to preach good news to the poor.... Isaiah 61:1 (NIV)

Take Us To The River

Words and Music by
ROBIN MARK

10
a song of Your sal - va - tion to win this gen-er-a -
en, for that cry is mer - cy, mer - cy to the
D
14
tion for our King; A song of Your for - give - ness,
fall-en sons of men; Mer-cy, it has tri - umphed,
G
A
G
for it is with grace that riv-er flows; Take us to the riv -
tri-umphed o-ver judg-ment by Your blood; Take us to the throne
D
F♯m
G

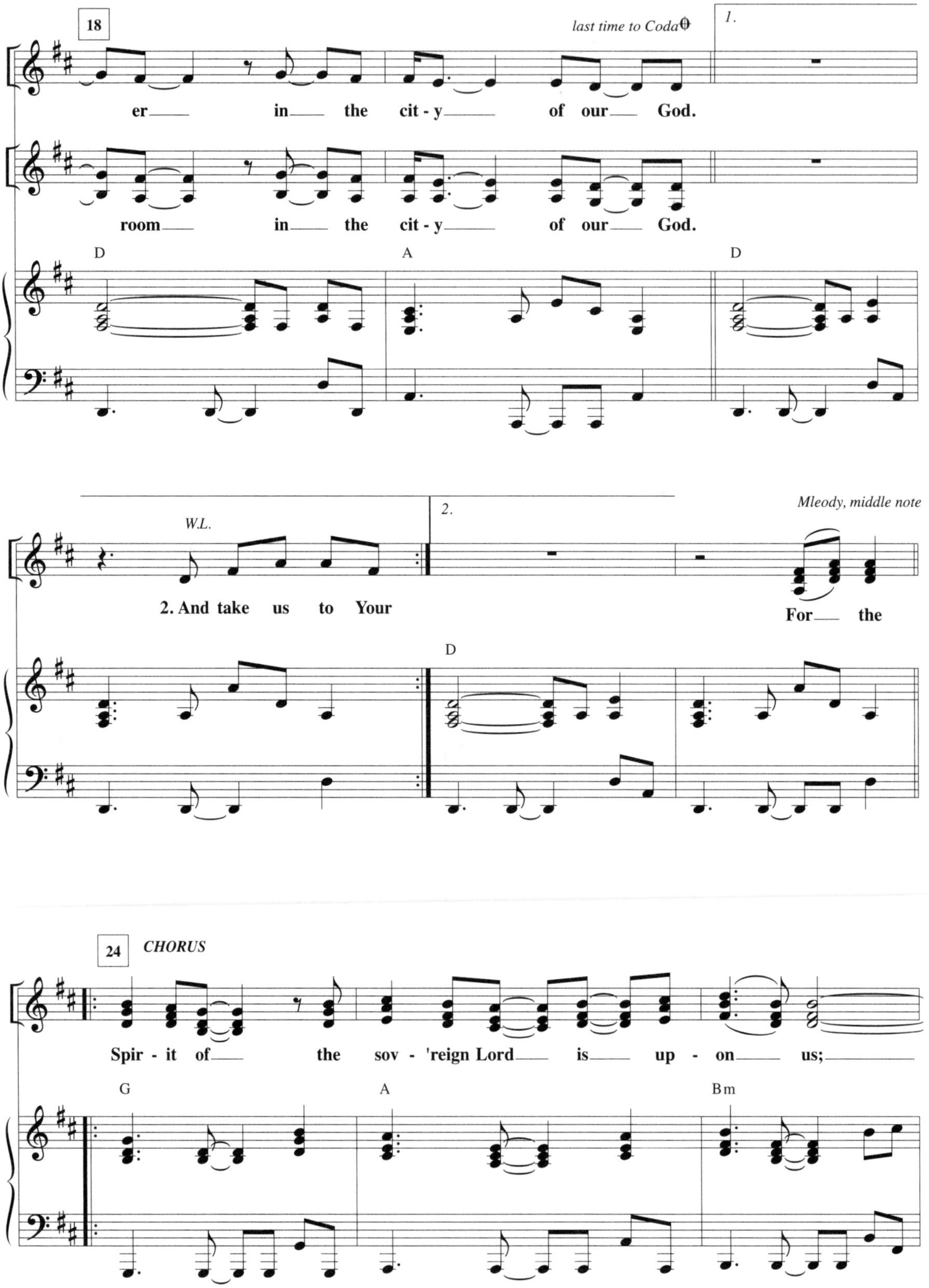

18

last time to Coda

1.

er in the cit - y of our God.

room in the cit - y of our God.

D A D

W.L.

2.

Mleody, middle note

2. And take us to Your

For the

D

28
This is the year of the
Bm7
G
D
32
Lord;
The Spir - it of the
A
A2
G
sov - 'reign Lord is up - on us;
A
Bm
Bm7
36
This is the year of the Lord;
G
D
A

1.
40
D
A
44
D
3. Take us to the moun -
48
VERSE 3
D
G
tain,
lift us in the shad - ow of Your hand;

52
Is this Your might-y an - gel who stands a-stride the
D
o-cean and the land; In his hand Your mer - cy
56
Small group
mer - cy;
G
A
G
show-ers o'er a dry and bar-ren place; Take us to the moun -
D
F♯m
G

60
tain in the ci - ty of our God.
D
A
D
For the
2.
D.S. al Coda
Take us to the riv -
Coda
D
Take us to the riv -
67
er in the cit - y of our God.
D
A

Medley options: Ancient Of Days.

1327

The city does not need the sun or the moon to shine on it, for the glory of God gives it light, and the Lamb is its lamp. Revelation 21:23 (NIV)

That City

Words and Music by
JOHN & ANNE BARBOUR

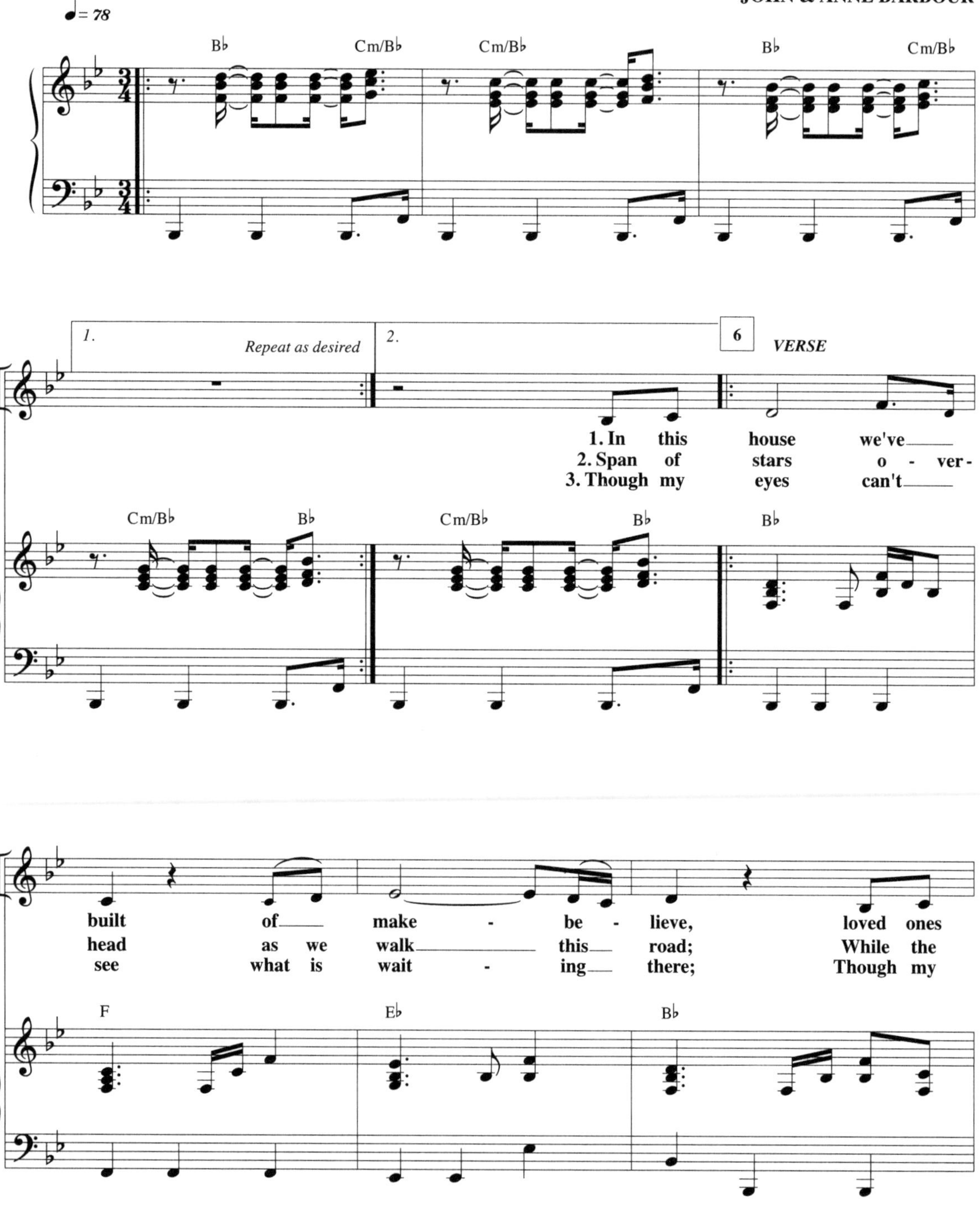

♩ = 78

B♭ Cm/B♭ Cm/B♭ B♭ Cm/B♭

1. Repeat as desired 2.

6 VERSE

1. In this house we've
2. Span of stars o - ver -
3. Though my eyes can't

Cm/B♭ B♭ Cm/B♭ B♭ B♭

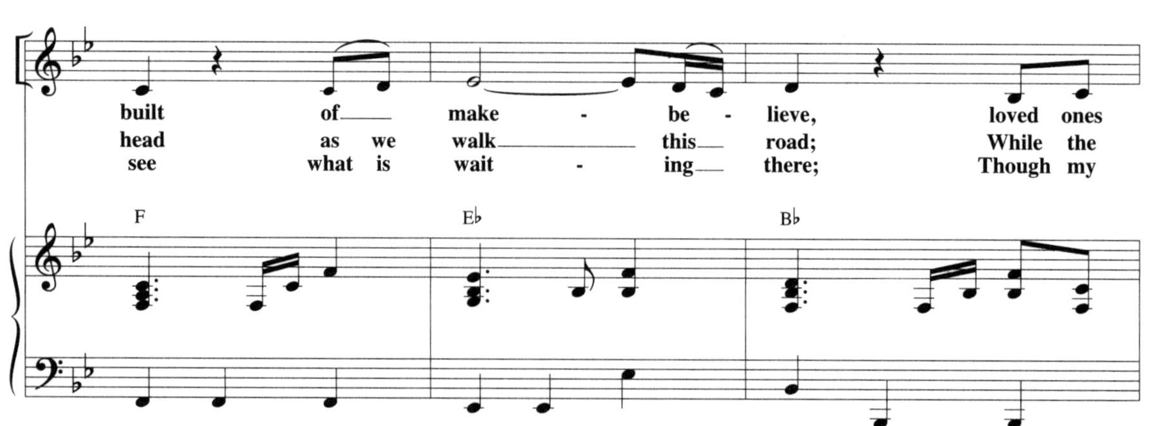

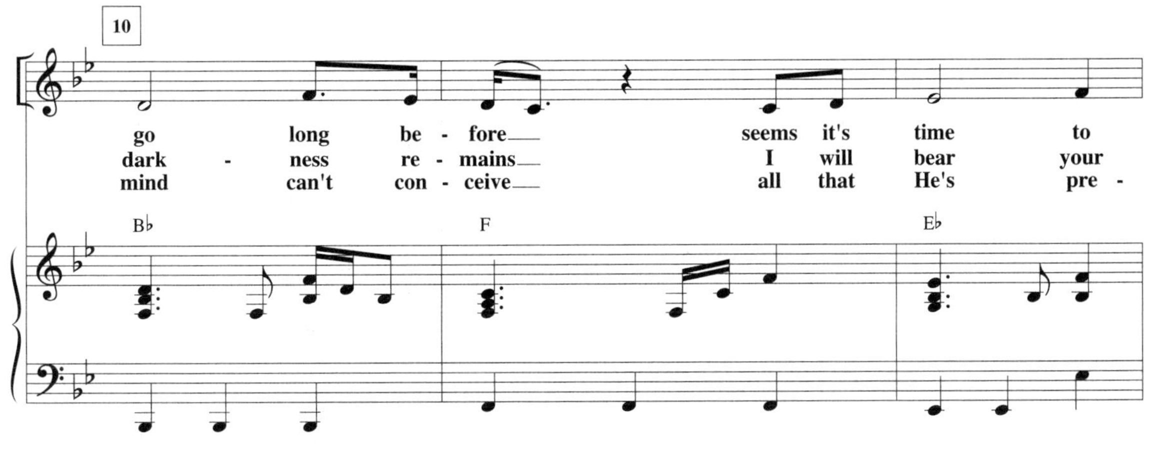
10
go long be - fore seems it's time to
dark - ness re - mains I will bear your
mind can't con - ceive all that He's pre -
B♭
F
E♭

14
leave; But we'll learn how to grieve, to for -
load; And to - geth - er we will tend the
pared; There the blind will see the sun, what was
F
B♭
E♭

18
give and re - ceive 'til we see them
seed He's sown as we walk a - long the
old will be young, and the lame, they will
B♭
F
D♭

1.
there in that ci - ty.
road to that ci - ty.
run in that ci - ty.
F
B♭
22
B♭
Cm/B♭
Cm/B♭
2, 3.
All
2. Span of
On that
B♭
Cm/B♭
Cm/B♭
B♭
B♭
27 CHORUS
day we will sing ho - ly, ho - ly;
B♭
E♭/B♭
B♭
E♭

31
On that day we'll bow down in the light;
B♭ E♭/B♭ B♭ F
35
And then we'll rise and
B♭ Cm7 B♭/D
39
turn our eyes to the One Who's the Light,
E♭ F/E♭ E♭ B♭/D
1.
the Light of that ci-ty.
F B♭ Cm/B♭ Cm/B♭

43
W.L.
2.
3. Though my
On that
B♭
Cm/B♭
Cm/B♭
B♭
F
46
CHORUS
W.L. ad libs
day we will sing ho - ly,
B♭
Cm7
B♭/D
E♭
50
On that day we'll bow down in the light;
B♭
54
And then we'll
F
B♭
Cm7

rise and turn our eyes to the One
Bb/D
Eb
F/Eb
Eb
58
Who's the Light,
1.
On that
2.
the Light of that
Bb/D
F
F
61
Sung 1st time only
W.L. ad libs
ci - ty.
Bb
Cm/Bb
Cm/Bb
Bb
Cm/Bb
Cm/Bb
Bb
Bb

1328

...."That all the kingdoms of the earth may know that You are the LORD God, You alone." 2 Kings 19:19 (NKJ)

That's My Lord

call up-on the One wound - ed for the lost. He rolled
He's the on-ly One Who does - n't have an end.
Cm7
Eb/F
14
CHORUS
Praise Team
W.L.
the stone a-way, that's my Lord; Set the pris-'ner free,
Bb
D7/F#
Gm
Eb
P.T.
18
All
that's my Lord; Let the wor-ship rise, let the peo-ple sing
a-bout the mer-cy of the Lamb Who is the King.
Bb/F
C9
1.

23
That's my Lord.
B♭
D7/F♯
Gm
E♭
2.
W.L.
Who is the King.
P.T.
Who is the King.
B♭
D7/F♯
Gm
E♭
E♭/F
D7/F♯
28
BRIDGE
W.L.
Let the prais-es of the saints of God rise up to His throne;
Gm
D
Gm7

32
Let the na - tions glo - ri - fy
Oo;
E♭
B♭/F
Gm7
D.S.
Him and Him a - lone.
Cause He rolled
Him and Him a - lone.
Cm7
Dsus
D
3.
All
38
W.L. ad libs
Optional: 1st time vocals only
P.T.
Who is the King.
That's my Lord,
E♭/F
B♭
D7/F♯
Gm
E♭

1.
Repeat as desired
That's my Lord.
B♭
D7/F♯
Gm
E♭
2.
He rolled
B♭
D7/F♯
Gm
E♭
44
CHORUS
P.T.
the stone a - way,
that's my Lord;
B♭
D7/F♯
Gm
E♭
W.L.
P.T.
48
W.L.
Set the pris-'ner free,
that's my Lord;
Let the wor-ship rise,
B♭
D7/F♯
Gm
E♭
B♭
D7/F♯
Gm

Medley options: Sing Out; Made Up Mind.

1329

The name of the LORD is a strong tower; the righteous run to it and are safe. Proverbs 18:10 (NIV)

This Love

Words and Music by
MIKE MOTLEY

10
You have made my life com - plete,
Noth - ing else com - pares to You,
A2
hear me when I say;
hear me when I say;
D2
14 All
I am fall - ing more
I am fall - ing more
E
in love with You;
in love with You,
F♯m7
D2
18
I am fall - ing more in love with You.
I am fall - ing more in love with You.
E
F♯m7
D

22
CHORUS
I will run in - to Your arms,
A
F♯m7
26
this is all I want,
You are all I need;
E
30
You, You're all
D2
A
I'm liv - ing for, all that I a - dore;
F♯m7

34
last time to Coda
Ev - 'ry-thing I need I
E
Bm7
1.
38
find in You.
D
A
W.L.
2.
W.L.
2. I'm find in
D2
D
43
BRIDGE
Sing 1st time only
P.T.
You. I find in You;
F♯m
E/G♯
D

47
W.L. ad libs
1.
P.T.
I find in You;
F♯m
E/G♯
D
2.
52
I find in You.
E/G♯
D
54
INSTRUMENTAL
A
F♯m7

E

D2
1.
D
2.
D.S. al Coda
D

Coda
64 CHORUS
find; I will run in - to Your arms,
D
A

68
this is all I want,
F♯m7
E

You are all I need;
E
D2
72
You, You're all I'm liv - ing for,
A
F♯m7
76
all that I a - dore;
Ev - 'ry-thing I
E
80
need I find,
I find in You;
Bm7
D

Medley options: For The Lord Is Good (DESHAZO/SADLER); I Love To Be In Your Presence.

...To him who sits on the throne and to the Lamb be praise and honor and glory and power, for ever and ever! Rev. 5:13 (NIV)

To Him Who Sits Upon The Throne

Words and Music by
DAVID CLIFTON and NICK HEBERT

or and all pow'r, A - men;
Cm7 Gm E♭ F Cm7
13
1st time WL middle note, Female soloist bottom note
2nd time WL middle note, PT harmonies
The Spir - it and the Bride say come, come to the Lamb,
Gm E♭ F Cm7 Gm E♭ F
17
the Liv - ing Wa - ter and the
Cm7 Gm E♭ F E♭
Ris - en Son.
Cm7 Fsus F

21
CHORUS
All, Melody top note
Who was and is and is to come, let ev - 'ry tribe
B♭ F E♭ F B♭ F
and ev - 'ry tongue lift up your voice and praise the
25
E♭ F B♭ F E♭
Ho - ly One.
1.
29
Cm7 Fsus F Gm E♭ F
P.T. 1st time only
Ah;
Cm7 Gm E♭ F

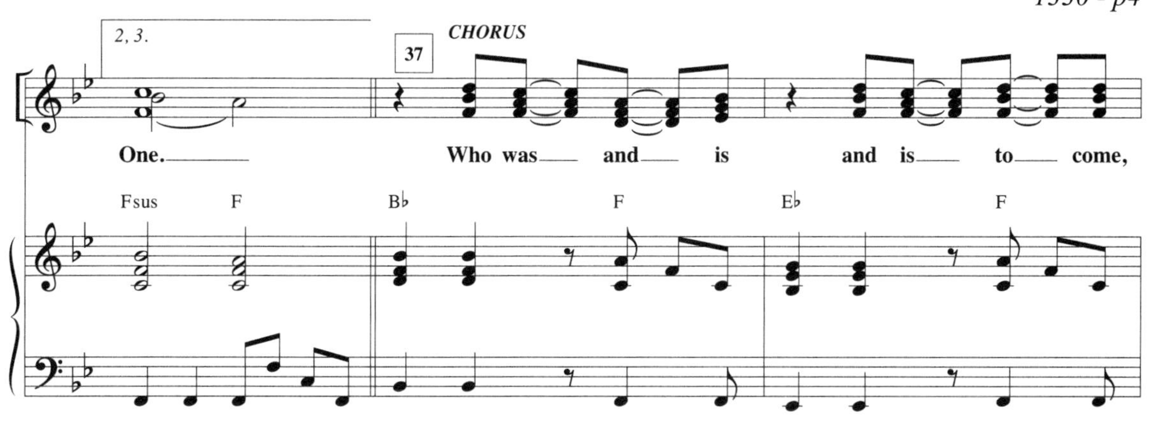
2, 3.
37
CHORUS
One.
Who was and is and is to come,
Fsus F Bb F Eb F

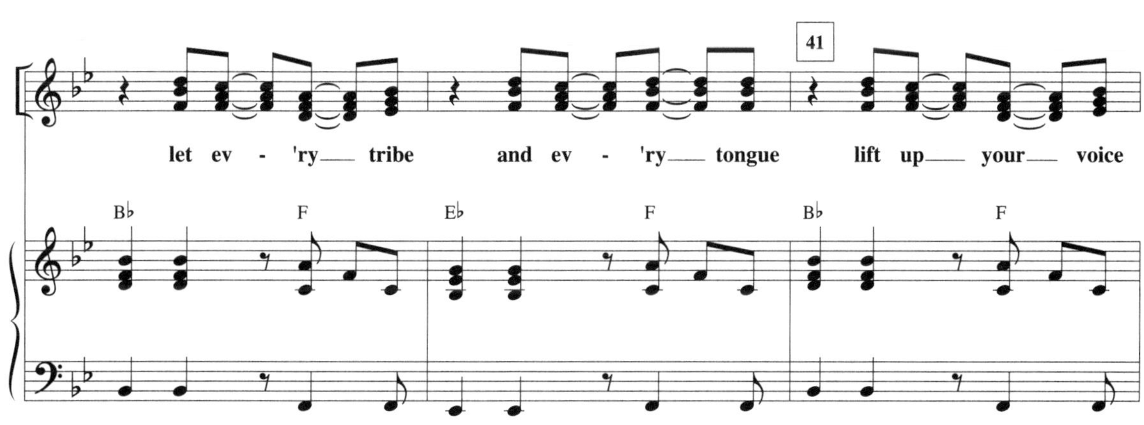
let ev - 'ry tribe and ev - 'ry tongue lift up your voice
Bb F Eb F
41
Bb F

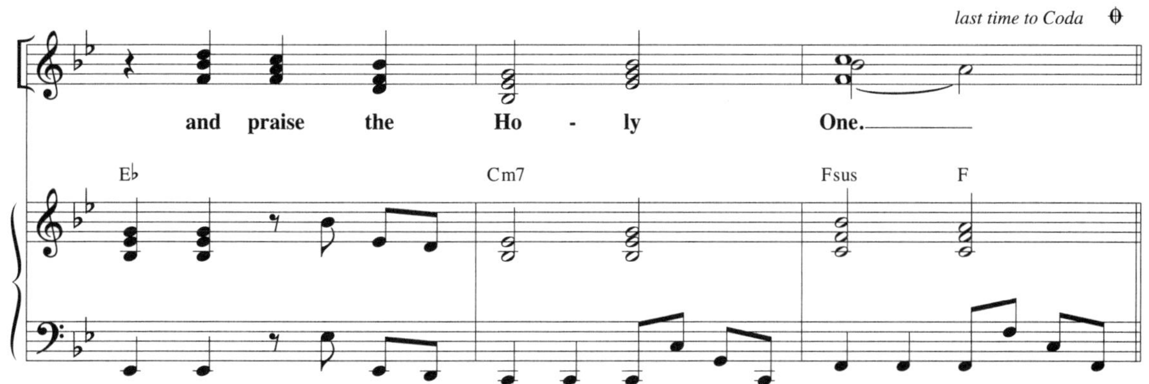
last time to Coda
and praise the Ho - ly One.
Eb Cm7 Fsus F

45

BRIDGE

W.L. & P.T. Men

Lord God Al - might - y, You are Ho - ly;

P.T.

Lord God Al - might - y, You are Ho - ly;

Gm Eb F Cm7 Gm Eb F

49

Lord God Al - might - y, You are Ho - ly.

1.

Lord God Al - might - y, You are;

Gm Eb F Cm7 Gm Eb F

2.
All
D.S. al Coda
y, You are Ho - ly.
ly;
Cm7
Cm7
Fsus
F
Coda CHORUS
Who was and is and is to come, let ev - 'ry tribe
B♭
F
E♭
F
B♭
F
57
and ev - 'ry tongue lift up your voice and praise the
E♭
F
B♭
F
E♭

61
Ho - ly One;
Who was and is
Cm7
Fsus
F
B♭
F
and is to come, let ev - 'ry tribe and ev - 'ry tongue
E♭
F
B♭
F
E♭
F
65
lift up your voice and praise the
B♭
F
E♭
69
Sung 1st time only
Ho - ly One.
Cm7
Fsus
F
Gm
E♭
F

Medley options: Jesus Christ Is Lord.

1331

...Present your bodies a living sacrifice, holy, acceptable to God, which is your reasonable service. Romans 12:1 (NKJ)

Two Hands, One Heart

10
I'll give my heart, not just a part, I'm lift-ing up my eve-ry-thing;
You made this heart, You made these hands, take me and use me as I am;
F
C
Dm
Eb/Bb
Bb
F/A
All
14
Well, it's all I have to of-fer, and it's all I have to give.
Well, it's all I have to of-fer, and it's all I have to give.
Gm7
F/A
Bbm7
Db/Eb
18
CHORUS
3rd time drums only
Two hands, one heart, one life to of-
Db6/Ab
Ab
Edim7
Fm
Db
Ab/C

22
3rd time band reenters
fer — You; Two hands, — one heart, —
D♭ E♭ D♭6/A♭ A♭ Edim7 Fm
last time to Coda
1.
that's what — I give — to You.
D♭ A♭/C B♭m7 E♭ A♭(add2)
E♭/G A♭
29
BRIDGE
Lit-tle be-comes — a lot when it's in — Your hands; Take me and make me more
Fm Fm/E♭ B♭/D

33
like — You; Well, it may not seem — like much, but with the Mast - er's touch,
D♭ E♭
Fm
Fm/E♭
D.S. al Coda
I know that I'll be more like — You. I have
B♭/D
D♭ E♭
D♭/E♭
39
CHORUS
All
Coda
W.L.
— to You. I have two hands, — one heart, —
B♭m E♭ A♭
D♭/A♭
Edim7 Fm
43
one life — to of - fer — You; Two hands, —
D♭ A♭/C
D♭ E♭
D♭6/A♭ A♭

Medley options: I Will Run To You.

Be still before the LORD and wait patiently for him... Psalm 37:7 (NIV)

We Wait

Words and Music by
WES TUTTLE

all our cares and wor - ries we
for Your might - y wind to car - ry us in -
D A/C♯ Bm D/A Em7
lay a - side for You;
All
O, how we long
to Your pres - ence, Lord;
And as we fill
A A♯dim7 Bm
to see Your face;
this house with praise;
F♯m7 Em7 A A♯dim7

last time to Coda
O, how we long for Your em-brace.
Let Your ho-ly fire - (re) fill this place.
Bm
F♯m7
Em7
2.
1. We wait,
As we wait,
A 7sus
A
A 7sus
A
D
A/C♯
1.
we wait;
We wait;
Bm
D/A
Em7
Gmaj7/A
A

2.
And as we fill this house with praise;
A
A♯dim7
Bm
F♯m7
Let Your holy fire-
Em7
A
A♯dim7
Bm
(re) fill this place.
As we wait,
F♯m7
Em7
A 7sus
A
we wait;
D
A/C♯
Bm
A

Medly options: My Heart, Your Home; You Are Here.

1333

....Worthy is the Lamb that was slain to receive power, and riches, and wisdom, and strength, and honour, and glory, and blessing. Revelation 5:12 (KJV)

What The Lord Has Done In Me

Words and Music by
REUBEN MORGAN

10
rich, let the blind say I can see, it's what the
way; From the heav - ens, mer - cy streams of the
Am G C G C
Both times All
16
Lord has done in me; Let the weak say I am
Sav - ior's love for me; I will rise from wa - ters
Dm7 G C C G
strong, let the poor say I am rich, let the
deep in - to the sav - ing arms of God; I will
C F G Am G
20
blind say I can see, it's what the Lord has done in
sing sal - va - tion songs; Je - sus Christ has set me
C G C Dm7 G

All
me.
free.
Ho -
C
25
CHORUS
san - na, ho - san - na to the Lamb that was
G
Am
F
29
Melody middle note
slain; Ho - san - na, ho - san - na, Je - sus
C
G
Em7
Am
G/B
Melody top note
33
died and rose a - gain; Ho - san - na, ho -
C
G
C
G

san - na to the Lamb that was slain; Ho -
Am
F
C
37
Melody middle note
san - na, ho - san - na, Je - sus died and rose a -
G
Em7
Am
G/B
C
G
1.
Ladies add harmony
2.
D.S.
gain;
2. In - to the
gain.
Ho -
C
C
3.
44
Worship Leader
gain;
1. Let the
C

Medley options: I Will Come And Bow Down; Come Thou Fount Of Every Blessing.

My soul thirsts for God, for the living God... Psalm 42:2 (NIV)

When All Is Said And Done

Words and Music by
TOMMY WALKER

CHORUS
1st time W.L. only
2nd time All
10
All that I long for, all that I hope for, is just that sense of You com - ing near;
E♭
B♭
Fm7
E♭/G
14
Last time to Coda
All that my heart is hun - gry to have is
A♭
E♭
B♭
18
just one more touch from Your lov - ing hand; When all is said and done,
Fm7
E♭/G
A♭
E♭
1, 2.
All
Lord, You're all I want. When
B♭
A♭

3.
Repeat as desired
Last time D.S. al Coda
Ab
Bb/Ab
Ab
Ab
Bb/Ab
Coda
28
CHORUS
just one more touch from Your lov - ing hand;
All that I long for,
Fm7
Eb/G
Ab
Eb
all that I hope for, is just that sense of You com - ing near;
Bb
Fm7
Eb/G
Ab
32
All that my heart is hun - gry to have is just one more touch from Your lov -
Eb
Bb
Fm7
Eb/G

Medley options: I Need You More; Lord, I Thirst For You.

...Bring me to your holy mountain, to the place where you dwell. Psalm 43:3 (NIV)

Where You Are

Words and Music by
TOMMY WALKER and JERRY WATTS

2nd time Men add duet
first, add all things to us, 'cause
flees, and all Your glo - ry's seen; Where You
go, and there is pure re - lease; In this
Gm/B♭ Gm7 F/G C 7sus
13
where You are, life's great - est joy is
live, O Lord, Your sweet de - li - v'rance
ho - ly place, our faith in You grows
F Dm
17
found; Our hun - gry souls are fed, our deep - est
flows, and where You dwell, there's love and
strong, to see Your heal - ing pow'r with grace and
B♭ F/B♭ Gm/B♭

All
1st time melody only

21 **CHORUS**

long - ings met.
bless - ed hope.
mer - cy fall.

Where You are,

Gm7 F/G C 7sus B♭2/D

where You are, where You are,

C/E B♭2/D C/E

25 27 *last time to Coda* 𝄌

O Lord, right here where You are.

B♭2/D C/E B♭/F

1 *All*

2. In Your

2. *D.S. al Coda*
Soloist

3. Where

F F F

Coda
34
INSTRUMENTAL
G
Em
38
C
G/C
Am/C
1.
2.
All
Where You are,
Am7
G/A
D 7sus
D 7sus
43
CHORUS
where You are,
C2/E
D/F#
C2/E

Medley options: Jesus, Lover Of My Soul; Bow Down.

After this I will return and will rebuild the tabernacle of David, which has fallen down; I will rebuild its ruins, and I will set it up. Acts 15:16 (NKJ)

Yahweh

Words and Music by
LEONARD JONES

W.L.
weh, come and dance with her a-gain;
W.L.
weh, Son of Dav-id, take Your place;
Am
G
13
All
Yah-weh, Yah-weh,
W.L.
come and make of both of us one new
All
Yah-weh, Yah-weh,
W.L. and Male Soloist
let us see the beau-ty of the Lord
Dm7
Am
G
17
All, melody bottom note
1.
land,
Yah-weh.
All, melody bottom note
to-day,
Yah-
Dm7
F
G

2, 3.
20
CHORUS
All
W.L.
weh. O, let the sun
G
C
C/E
shine a - gain,
24
on the streets
G
Dm
of Je - ru - sa - lem;
W.L.
O,
Am
F
28
All
let the sun
shine a - gain,
C
C/E
G

32
on the streets
of Je -
Dm
ru - sa - lem
O,
Am
F
1.
2.
D.S.
F
3.
38
F
Am
Repeat as desired

Medley options: We Have Overcome (KERR/MERKEL); Shalom Jerusalem.

...For you alone are holy. All nations will come and worship before you... Revelation 15:4 (NIV)

You Alone

Words and Music by
CLINT BROWN

de - serve my praise;
B♭/D
Fsus
F
17
1st time W.L.
2nd time Ladies add harmony
So I come be - fore You, I hon - or and a - dore
B♭
Cm7
F
You;
21
W.L.
You a - lone are wor - thy of my
B♭
Cm7
B♭/D
praise, on - ly You a - lone.
1.
Fsus
F
B♭
E♭/B♭

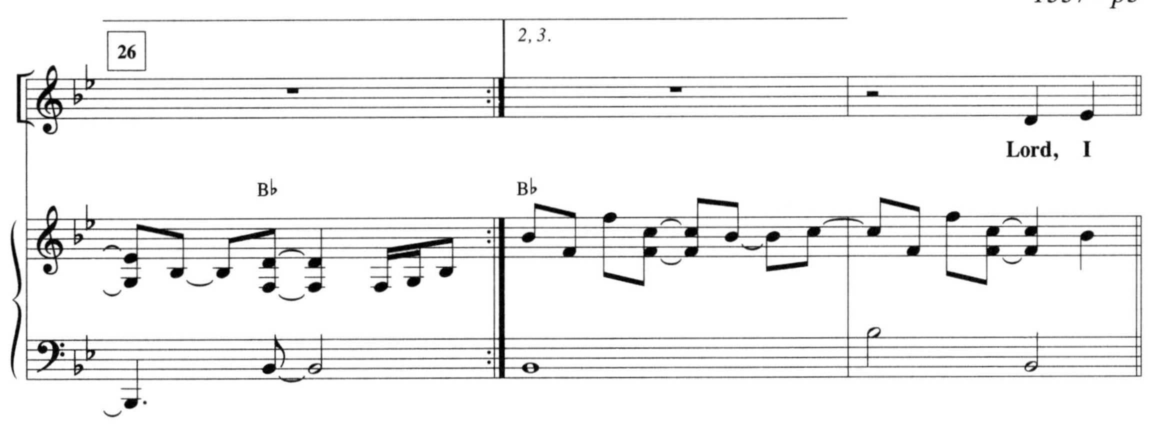
26
2, 3.
B♭
B♭
Lord, I

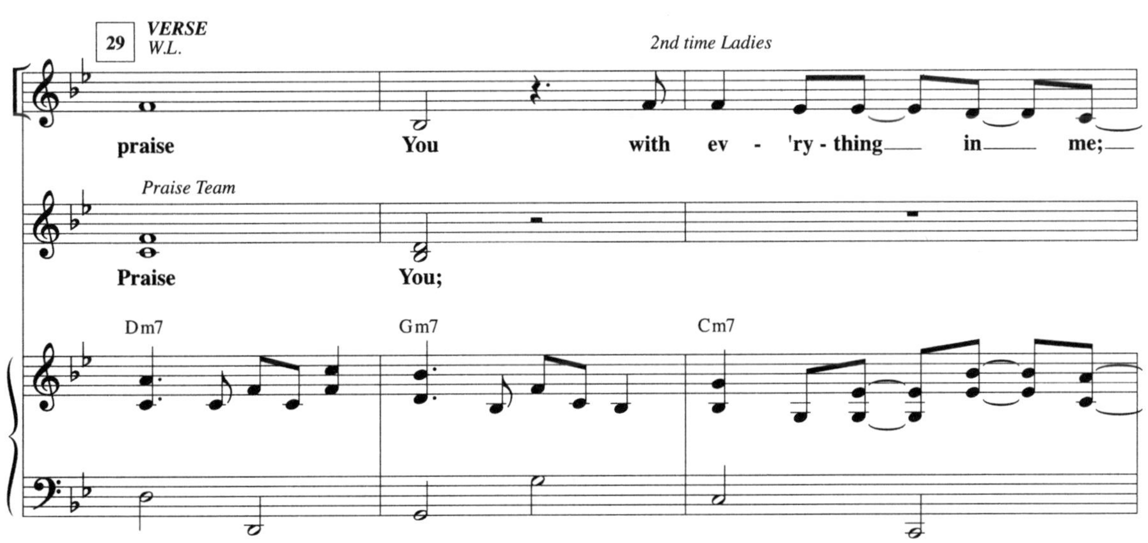
29
VERSE
W.L.
2nd time Ladies
praise You with ev - 'ry - thing in me;
Praise Team
Praise You;
Dm7
Gm7
Cm7

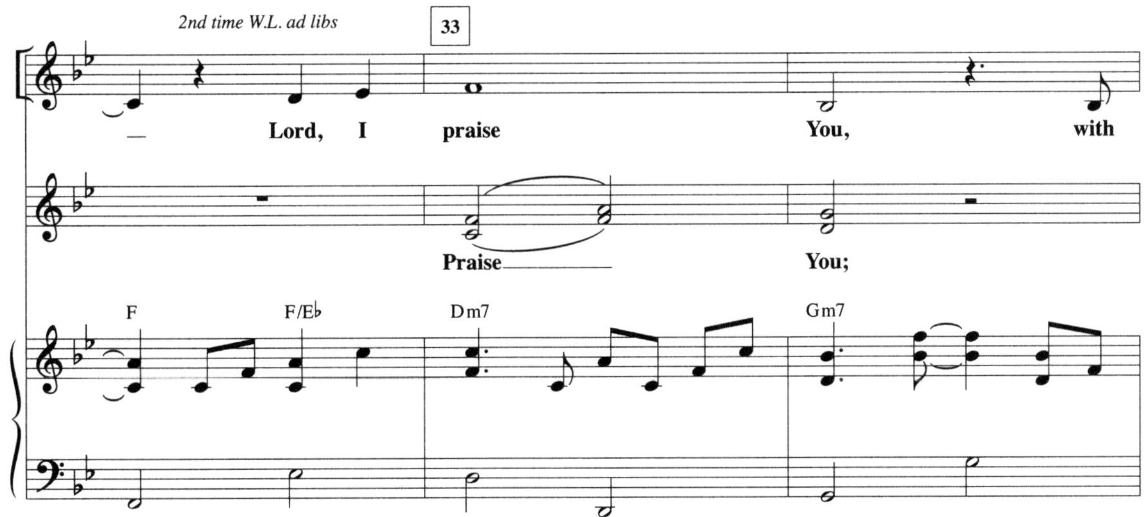
2nd time W.L. ad libs
33
Lord, I praise You, with
Praise You;
F
F/E♭
Dm7
Gm7

36
W.L.
1.
hon - or I will sing.
Cm7
Fsus
F
2.
40
P.T.
You a - lone are ho -
F
G 7sus
C
W.L. ad libs
ly;
You a - lone are wor - thy;
Dm7
G
C
44
You a - lone;
Dm7
C/E
Gsus

48
So I come before You,
G
C
Dm7
hon - or and a - dore You;
52
You a - lone.
G
C
Dm7
C/E
Gsus
G
1.
2.
57
on - ly You a - lone.
G
C
Dm7

Medley options: Rest In Your Love; Center Of My Joy.

O God, you are my God, earnestly I seek you... Psalm 63:1 (NIV)

You Are

Words and Music by
CLINT BROWN

2nd time add W.L.
more than this world to me; I would-n't trade You for sil-ver or gold;
Gb/Ab
Db
Ab/C

14
I would-n't trade You for rich-es un-told; You are,
Bbm7(add4)
Db2/Ab
Gb2

17
1.
You are my ev' - ry - thing.
Ab7sus
Db
Ab7sus

2, 3.
21
VERSE
Female soloist
1. I would-n't take one step
W.L.
2. Un - til the world
Db
Ebm7
Db/F
Gbmaj7
with - out You;
I could nev-er go on;
stops turn-ing,
un-til the stars
fade from the sky,
Fm7
Bbm7
Ebm7
Gb/Ab
Db
Ebm7
Db2/F
25
I could-n't live one day with-out You;
W.L. & Female soloist
un - til the sun stops ris - ing, I'll
Gbmaj7
Fm7
Bbm7

1.
I don't have the strength to make it on my own.
need You in my life, and
Ebm7
Db2/F
Gb
Ab7sus
2.
30
W.L. ad libs
here's the rea - son why.
You are.
Gb
Ab7sus
Eb
Bb/D
Ab2
Cm7
Bb7sus
34
Eb
Bb/D

Fm7(add4)
E♭/G
B♭7sus
38
CHORUS
1st time W.L. & Female soloist
2nd time All
You are the love of my life; You are the
E♭
B♭/D
Cm7(add4)
42
hope that I cling to; You mean more than this world to me;
E♭2/B♭
A♭2
A♭/B♭
All
46
I would-n't trade You for sil-ver or gold; I would-n't trade You for
E♭
B♭/D
Cm7(add4)

Medley options: More Of You (NYSTROM/HARRIS); I Love To Be With You.

Help me, O LORD my God! Oh, save me according to your mercy. PSALM 109:26 (NKJ)

Your Mercy Goes Much Deeper

Words and Music by
LINDELL COOLEY and LENNY LeBLANC

9
far-ther than I can see;
Your mer - cy goes much deep - er,
Your grace,
far-ther than I can see;
Your mer - cy,
Your grace,
A♭/C
B♭/D
E♭
last time to Coda
it res - cues me;
Your mer - cy goes much deep - er,
Your mer - cy;
A♭maj7
E♭
far - ther than I can see.
I
far - ther than I can see.
A♭/C
B♭/D
E♭

14
VERSE
W.L.
reach for You when I'm go - ing un - der; I wait for You,
A♭ Cm7 Fm7 E♭/G A♭ A♭ Cm
17
1.
2.
Molto rit.
W.L.
Je - sus, You're my life - line. Your mer- line. Where could I
P.T.
Your mer–
Fm7 E♭/G A♭ B♭sus B♭ B♭sus B♭
20
BRIDGE
A tempo
1st time W.L. only; 2nd time add harmonies
go, where would I stand; How could I
Praise Team, 2nd time only
Where could I go, stand; How could I
Cm A♭ E♭/B♭ B♭ Gm7

leave the shel - ter of Your hand; Where could I
leave the shel - ter of Your hand;
Cm
Fm7
B♭
Gm7
24
go, where would I stand; How could I
Where could I go, stand; How could I
Cm
A♭
E♭/B♭
B♭
Gm7
3
1.
leave the shel - ter of Your hand.
leave the shel - ter.
Cm
Fm7
Gsus
G

27
INSTRUMENTAL
Cm
A♭
E♭/B♭
B♭
Gm7

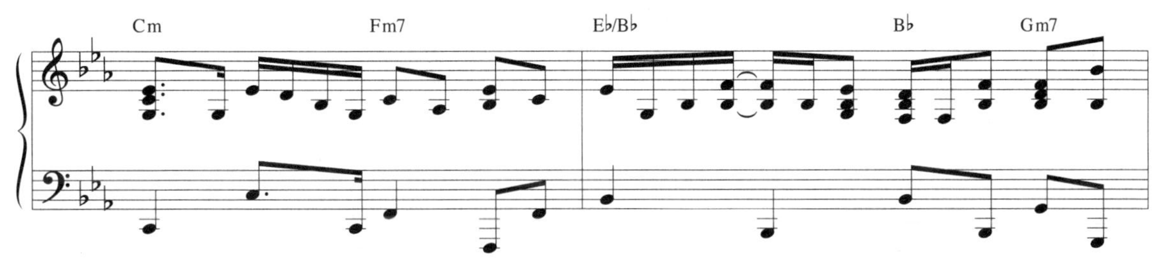
Cm
Fm7
E♭/B♭
B♭
Gm7

31
Cm
A♭
E♭/B♭
B♭
Gm7
Cm
Fm7

All
2.
D.S. al Coda
Where could I
hand.
Your mer–
Gsus
G
Gsus
G

Coda

Medley options: I Need You More; Lord, You Have My Heart.

On his robe and on his thigh he has this name written: KING OF KINGS AND LORD OF LORDS. Rev. 19:16 (NIV)

You're The Lion Of Judah

Words and Music by
ROBIN MARK

10
end of the age, when the earth You re - claim, You will
Fa - ther has told us for these You have died, for the
D
G
D
gath - er the na - tions be - fore You; And the
na - tions that ga - ther be - fore You and the
All
A
2
14
eyes of all men will be fixed on the Lamb Who was
ears of all men need to hear of the Lamb Who was
18
cru - ci - fied; With wis - dom and mer - cy and
cru - ci - fied, Who de - scend - ed to hell, yet was
G
D
A

W.L.
jus - tice You'll reign at Your Fa - ther's side. And the
raised up to reign at His Fa - ther's side.
A
G
A
22 CHORUS
All
an - gels will cry, Hail the Lamb,
D
G
D/F♯
A
W.L.
26
All
Who was slain for the world, rule in
D
G
D/F♯
W.L.
30
pow'r And the earth will re - ply,
A
D

All
You shall reign as the
G D/F♯ A
34
King of all kings and the
1.
Lord of all lords.
D G D/F♯ Em7 D
All
2.) There's a
G/D D Dsus2,4 D G/D D Dsus2,4
2.
41
Lord of all lords.
G D/F♯ Em7 D G D

G
A
D
G
D
All
49
And the eyes of all men will be fixed on the Lamb Who was
A
2
A
53
cru - ci - fied; With wis - dom and mer - cy and
G
D
A
D.S.
jus - tice You'll reign at Your Fa - ther's side. And the
G
A

3.
W.L.
58
CHORUS
All
Lord of all Lords. And the an - gels will cry, Hail the
G D/F♯ Em7 D
D
G D/F♯
Lamb, Who was slain for the world,
W.L.
62
A
2
D
All
rule in pow'r
W.L.
And the
G D/F♯
A
2
66
earth will re - ply,
All
You shall reign
D
G D/F♯
A

Medley options: Shout To The North; Be Exalted.

INDEX A
INDEX ACCORDING TO KEY AND TEMPO

C MAJOR, cont'd

C MINOR

C-SHARP MINOR

D MAJOR

D MINOR

D-FLAT MAJOR

E MAJOR

E MAJOR, cont'd

E MINOR

E-FLAT MAJOR

F MAJOR

F MINOR

G MAJOR

G MAJOR, cont'd

Moderate

Slow

G MINOR

Fast

INDEX B
TOPICAL INDEX

ADORATION

ASSURANCE

BLOOD OF CHRIST

CALL TO WORSHIP

COMMITMENT

CONSECRATION

DECLARATION

DECLARATION, Cont'd

EVANGELISM

GOD, THE FATHER

HEALING

HOLY SPIRIT

JESUS, THE SON

JOY

PRAISE

TESTIMONY

THANKSGIVING

VICTORY

WORD OF GOD

INDEX C
INDEX ACCORDING TO FIRST LINES

INDEX D
INDEX ACCORDING TO SCRIPTURE REFERENCE

INDEX E
INDEX OF COPYRIGHT OWNERS

Barbour Cuts Music, Inc., c/o Lori Kelly Rights & Licenses, 1190 Laurel Fig Dr., Simi Valley, CA 93063: Selection 1327.

Darlene Zschech/Hillsong Publishing, (adm in the U.S. and Canada by Integrity's Hosanna! Music) c/o Integrity Music Inc., 1000 Cody Road, Mobile, AL 36695: Selection 1325.

Crooked Letter Music, (adm in the U.S. and Canada by Integrity's Praise! Music) c/o Integrity Music, Inc., 1000 Cody Rd., Mobile, AL 36695: Selection 1304.

David Binion Music, c/o Gaither Copyright Management, P.O. Box 737, Alexandria, IN 46001: Selection 1322.

Daybreak Music, Ltd, (administered in the U.S. and Canada by Integrity's Hosanna! Music) c/o Integrity Music, Inc., 1000 Cody Rd., Mobile, AL 36695: Selections 1314, 1340.

Doulos Publishing, (adm by The Copyright Company, Nashville, TN) c/o The Copyright Company, 40 Music Square East, Nashville, TN 37203: Selection 1289.

Eaglestar Productions, c/o Morningstar Publications, 4803 W. US Highway 421, Wilkesboro, NC 28697: Selections 1274, 1336.

Integrity's Alleluia! Music, c/o Integrity Music, Inc., 1000 Cody Road, Mobile, AL 36695: Selections 1270, 1287.

Integrity's Hosanna! Music, c/o Integrity Music, Inc., 1000 Cody Road, Mobile, AL 36695: Selections 1267, 1269, 1272, 1273, 1274, 1275, 1276, 1277, 1278, 1279, 1280, 1283, 1284, 1286, 1288, 1291, 1295, 1297, 1298, 1299, 1300, 1305, 1306, 1307, 1308, 1309, 1310, 1313, 1315, 1317, 1318, 1320, 1321, 1324, 1328, 1329, 1330, 1331, 1332, 1335, 1339.

Integrity's Praise! Music, c/o Integrity Music, Inc., 1000 Cody Road, Mobile, AL 36695: Selections 1271, 1282, 1290, 1292, 1293, 1294, 1296, 1301, 1302, 1303, 1304, 1312, 1316, 1334, 1335.

Interior Music Corp., 5750 Wilshire Blvd., Suite 565-W, Los Angeles, CA 90036: Selection 1285.

Juniper Landing Music, c/o ROM Administration, P.O. Box 1252, Fairhope, AL 36533: Selections 1288, 1291, 1321, 1331.

Kingsway's Thank You Music, c/o EMI Christian Music Publishing, 101 Winners Circle, P.O. Box 5085, Brentwood, TN 37024-5085: Selection 1326.

LenSongs Publishing, 287 Spout Springs Road, Muscle Shoals, AL 35661: Selections 1280, 1295, 1308, 1317, 1328, 1339.

Music Missions Publishing, c/o Music Missions International, P.O. Box 9788, Pensacola, FL 32513: Selections 1276, 1280, 1295, 1308, 1315, 1317, 1328, 1329, 1339.

Reuben Morgan/Hillsong Publishing, (adm in the U.S. and Canada by Integrity's Hosanna! Music) c/o Integrity Music Inc., 1000 Cody Road, Mobile, AL 36695: Selection 1333.

Ron Kenoly Music, c/o FranAm Publishing, 1608 Cahuenga Blvd, Suite 203, Hollywood, CA 90028: Selection 1319.

Ruminating Music/IQ Music Ltd., c/o Wixen Music Publishing, 23564 Calabasas Rd. #107, Calabasas, CA 91302-1337: Selection 1330.

Sheep In Tow Music, c/o Copyright Management Services, Inc., 1625 Broadway, 4th Floor, Nashville, TN 37203-3138: Selection 1323.

Tribe Music Group, c/o Pypo Publishing, P.O. Box 607608, Orlando, FL 32860: Selections 1322, 1337, 1338.

We Mobile Music, (adm in the U.S. and Canada by Integrity's Praise! Music) c/o Integrity Music, Inc., 1000 Cody Rd., Mobile, AL 36695: Selections 1271, 1303.

worshiptogether.com songs/Six Steps Music, c/o EMI Christian Music Publishing, 101 Winners Circle, P.O. Box 5085, Brentwood, TN 37024-5085: Selection 1281.

Ylonek Music, c/o FranAm Publishing, 1608 Cahuenga Blvd, Suite 203, Hollywood, CA 90028: Selections 1268, 1311.